PURNELL LIBRARY OF KNOWLEDGE
Apes and Monkeys

Published in 1970 by Purnell

Made and printed in Italy.
SBN 361 01537 2

Apes and Monkeys

by Clive Roots

Illustrated by Richard Orr

Foreword by Dr. Maurice Burton,

PURNELL

London

Foreword
by Dr. Maurice Burton

Centuries ago learned men thought that animals had been created solely for man's benefit. One 16th century book states that some animals are there merely for man's amusement; two specially mentioned are apes and marmosets. Well, most of us would now agree that there is more to them than that. For one thing, several people have almost literally lived with troops of baboons, chimpanzees or gorillas. What they have to say as a result not only makes fascinating reading but has completely altered our ideas. Nowhere is this more true than with the gorilla.

When ships from Europe first sailed down the coast of West Africa seamen brought back stories of wild men living there. Later, explorers told horrifying tales of huge man-like apes, powerfully-built and savage, that were said to attack men and carry off women and children. And yet not many years ago a young woman spent months living in the forest side by side with gorillas and found them most peaceful, despite their strength.

The pity is that just as we are beginning to know these – our nearest relatives – really well, there are fears for their survival. These fears are very real. Tens of thousands of one species of monkey alone have been sent to laboratories. Capturing one gorilla or orang utan for a zoo has sometimes meant killing the rest of the family as they tried to defend it. Worst of all, the forests where these animals live are being destroyed.

It is good to be able to report signs of a change for the better. We cannot afford to lose these animals, if for no better reason than that in studying them we learn much that sheds light on our own behaviour. It would be ironic if future historians had to report that monkeys and apes were saved from destruction and in their turn, by the things they taught us, saved the human race from destroying itself.

This could well become true, although a long way ahead. Meanwhile let us enjoy, in the pages of this book, making the acquaintance of our cousins in the animal world.

Contents

Introduction

BEFORE we take a look at monkeys we should really understand how they came into being, and to do this we must investigate the whole animal kingdom, which includes all living creatures. For example, reptiles, mammals, birds – and even fish, insects and snails – are all animals. Mammals are the ones that are covered with fur (or quills or "armour plate"). With only two exceptions mammals give birth to live young, and they all suckle their young. They are divided into many orders, such as monkeys and their relatives, cats, dogs, rodents and so on.

Monkeys and their relatives all belong to the order known as the primates. "Monkey" is simply a rather loose name given to some primates – mainly those other than the primitive forms and the apes. In this book, therefore, all except the recognized monkeys will be referred to as primates.

Within any order there are usually many families. In the primates there are, for example, Baboons, Lemurs, Lorises, Apes and several others; and each family has a number of species.

All the primates alive today have developed and improved over millions of years from primitive insect-eating animals. These early ancestors bore little resemblance to the monkeys and apes of the present day, let alone to man – who is, after all, the most advanced primate and therefore the most intelligent animal. So when we talk about primitive primates, we mean primates of the earliest type.

The series of slow changes during which many animals die out as their homes are taken over by more advanced species, is known as evolution. How do we know about it? The answer lies in the work of palaeontologists. By studying the fossilized remains of animals, these scientists have been able to build up a picture of what life was like millions of years ago, and how animals evolved. Present-day animals are studied by zoologists, who relate their

Below: skull of Paleocene Prosimian. This creature lived between 60,000,000 and 50,000,000 years ago.

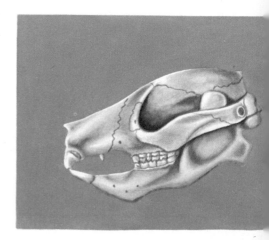

findings to those of the palaeontologists.

During the course of evolution all animals have become specialized at doing something. The primates could be said to have concentrated on brain development and intelligence; and as they did not have horns or "armour plate" for protection, they took to the trees to escape their enemies.

Another important point to remember is that evolution has taken many, many years – more, than we can really visualize. This planet is very old and animals have been on it for about one thousand million years. The most highly-developed animals – the mammals – have only been in existence for about seventy million years. In evolutionary terms, therefore, they are comparative babies.

Evolution can be explained visually as a kind of tree, with branches growing out from the main trunk showing where and when particular groups of animals branched off. If we give mammals a "tree" of their own we will see that the family of primates branched off very early in its growth. So, while primates are the most intelligent of all animals, they are certainly not the latest to develop.

This may all seem very confusing, so in order to make the monkey kingdom a little easier to understand, the actual order in which primates evolved is not strictly followed in this book.

Above: skeleton of Eocene Prosimian. Right: reconstruction of Eocene Prosimian. The Eocene epoch was between 50,000,000 and 30,000,000 years ago.

Left: Common Tree Shrew, which could possibly be the first in the long line of primates leading eventually to monkeys, apes, ape man and man himself. Below: the Lesser Tree Shrew. Fossils of Tree Shrews have been found in Mongolia that are little different from those animals alive today.

The first monkeys

The nest-makers

DURING evolution when animals branched off from one group to form another, more successful one, their more primitive ancestors did not necessarily become extinct. In fact, primitive primates still live on in many parts of the world – like the Tree Shrews, which live in the wooded areas of south east Asia, the islands of the Malay Archipelago and the Philippine and Nicobar islands. These are thought to look very similar to the animals that first emerged from the main tree of life to form the primate order. So if we could trace our development back for many millions of years we might find that our earliest ancestors were very like these small, squirrel-like animals, sitting on branches and holding food in their paws.

One of the most interesting things about Tree Shrews is that, like the Lemurs that followed a little later, they make a nest for their young. All the higher primates, on the other hand, carry their babies around with them, clinging to their backs or chests. Another unusual feature of Tree

Shrews is an ability to make a wide range of sounds, from shrill screams to bird-like twittering.

Tree Shrews hunt during the daytime, although hunt hardly describes their means of food-gathering as they eat virtually anything edible – not only fruit, leaves and buds but also frogs, insects, small lizards, eggs, young birds, snails and worms. At night they sleep curled up in their nests – or even, despite their name, in holes in the ground – with their bushy tails covering them like blankets. Although they are active during daylight, Tree Shrews have the large eyes characteristic of the "night shift" animals – but good sight is, of course, important to animals that live mainly in trees.

Tree Shrews have been included in the monkey kingdom because of their structure. Anatomists (who study body structure) were very surprised when they first made detailed examinations of these animals. They found they had the teeth of insectivores (true shrews, moles and hedgehogs), and in fact resembled the Elephant Shrew of Africa, yet their skull structure was that of the early primates as they had bony rings around their eyes. However, more recent discoveries indicate that perhaps it is wrong, after all, to include Tree Shrews among the primates. There is certainly still some confusion over their exact classification.

Above: Pen-tailed Shrew, a mouse-like creature with a primitive brain.
Below: chart showing areas of distribution of Tree Shrews, Tarsiers and Lorises in south east Asia.

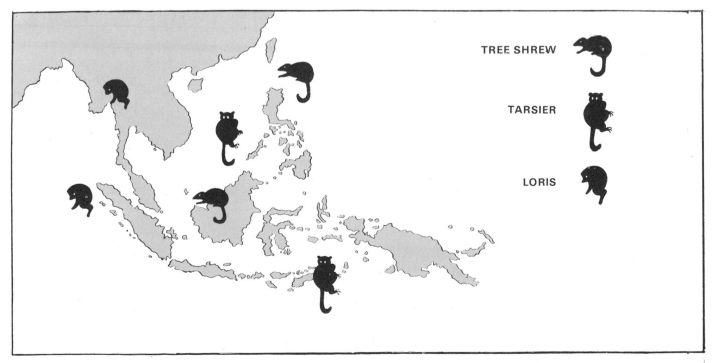

TREE SHREW

TARSIER

LORIS

14

Bushbabies on the branch of a tree. Trees are their natural habitat and they rarely descend to the ground. The lower animal is the Thick-tailed Bushbaby, and the upper one Demidoff's Bushbaby.

The night-shift

During the day the forest is a relatively quiet place, but when the brief tropical twilight gives way abruptly to darkness a new set of sounds breaks the stillness. In the equatorial jungles of Africa, Bushbabies and Pottos arouse themselves from their sleeping places in tree holes, and in the forests of Asia Lorises appear.

Bushbabies are probably the most familiar of the primitive primates, as they are attractive looking and have made many appearances on television. They are the very first of the primates to show a definite flattening of the face – a characteristic seen in its most extreme form in the higher primates, particularly in the apes and in man.

Bushbabies in their natural state live only in Africa, and the smallest species is Demidoff's Bushbaby. This is so tiny it can sit quite comfortably in a human hand, but despite its size it is an amazing jumper. The secret of this lies in extremely long ankle bones, resulting in three sections of bone between body and feet instead of the normal two such as we ourselves have. Bushbabies seldom venture to the ground, but when this is necessary they bounce along on their hind legs rather like miniature kangaroos.

The Thick-tailed Bushbaby is the largest species and is usually a bad-tempered animal, quite unsuitable for keeping as a pet. Even the most commonly kept species – the medium-sized Senegal Bushbaby – is a nocturnal animal which will sleep all day unless it is exceptionally hungry, so is hardly an ideal pet either. Also, all Bushbabies have the unusual habit of wetting on their hands and feet. In their natural habitat this marks out their territory and warns off other Bushbabies; however, it can be rather unpleasant if a Bushbaby is allowed to exercise in the house.

Bushbabies have enormous membranous ears to help them locate their insect prey in the dark (although they eat fruit, leaves, young birds and small lizards, too), and their fur is very thick to protect them from the cool dampness of the tropical night.

Bushbabies belong to the Loris family, but the other members of this group are in complete contrast, being slow and deliberate in their movements. There are only three species – the Slow Loris, the Lesser Slow Loris and the Slender Loris. The last lives only in southern India and Ceylon, and is usually a bad-tempered animal; when disturbed it becomes irritable and rocks from side to side, growling threateningly. It has very spindly legs, is mainly grey in colour and sleeps curled up in the tree tops during the daytime.

Above: Slender Loris. Below: Thick-tailed Bushbaby, which is the largest of the Bushbabies.

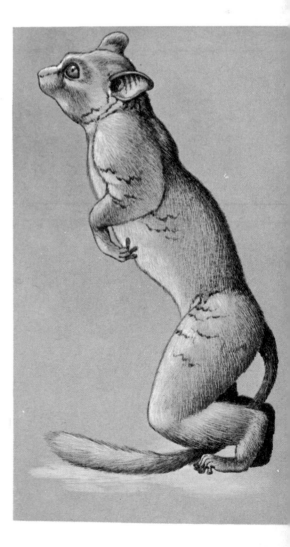

Slow Lorises, which live in the forests of south east Asia, are even more ponderous in their movements. However, they can swing their heads round with amazing speed to transfix anything that touches them with their very sharp teeth. To make matters worse, they have such a strong grip that once they have taken hold of anything it is difficult to prise them loose. Strong muscles, powerful thumbs and large toes contribute to this pincer-like grip, in the development of which these animals have practically lost their index fingers. Slow Lorises also have a specialized blood supply to their feet which allows them to hang on for a long time without tiring, even when hanging by one foot.

In Thailand people are very superstitious about the Slow Loris; and old sailing ships often carried one aboard to guard against being becalmed. The early Dutch colonists of the East Indian islands (now Indonesia) called this animal "loerus" which means clown, and from this has been derived its present name. The Slow Loris is larger and stockier than the Slender Loris but has smaller ears, and the young of both species are peculiar in having a full set of teeth at birth.

In Africa there are two species related to the Asiatic Lorises – the Potto and the strange Agwantibo. The Potto lives in the dense forests of central

Above: adult Slow Loris with baby clinging to her back. Young Lorises are more rusty in colouring than the adults. Left: Potto, who though he moves extremely slowly and carefully in his hunt for flies is usually successful in catching them. African folk tales suggest that by the time a Potto has moved from one tree to another he is in danger of starving to death.

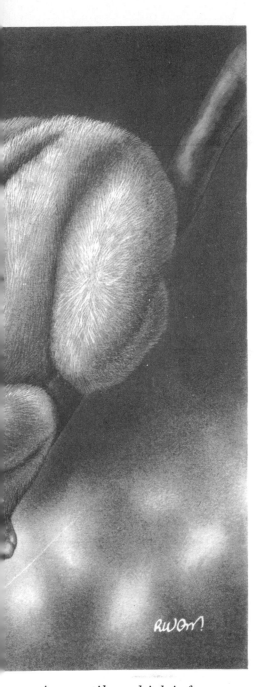

and west Africa, and looks rather like a Slow Loris except that it has a stumpy little tail, about one inch long, and a strange defence armament. Three of the Potto's vertebrae (the bones that make up the backbone) pierce the skin and are protected by a hard, horny covering. When attacked the Potto stretches up and flings itself forward, at the same time turning its head down so that the spikes strike the attacker in a downward motion. Like the Lorises, the Potto moves in a very ponderous manner, never jumping from branch to branch like a Bushbaby.

The Pottos and their relatives are still plentiful in the tropics with the exception of one species; this is the Agwantibo, which is smaller than the Potto and does not have an exposed backbone or a tail. It has the most pincer-like hands of all the Lorises, and its first and second fingers have practically disappeared.

It is only in recent years that Agwantibos have been kept in zoos in any numbers, and there they are housed in buildings known as noctural houses. During the day, when people are visiting the zoo, the animals are shown in subdued lighting that resembles their normal night-time conditions. At night full lighting is switched on to induce the Agwantibos, and the other Lorises, to think it is daytime and go to sleep.

Agwantibo, which is far more rare than the Potto and smaller in size. It is only found on the Calabar Coast of Nigeria. The Agwantibo shows a resemblance to the Slender Loris, while the Potto shows more likeness to the Slow Loris.

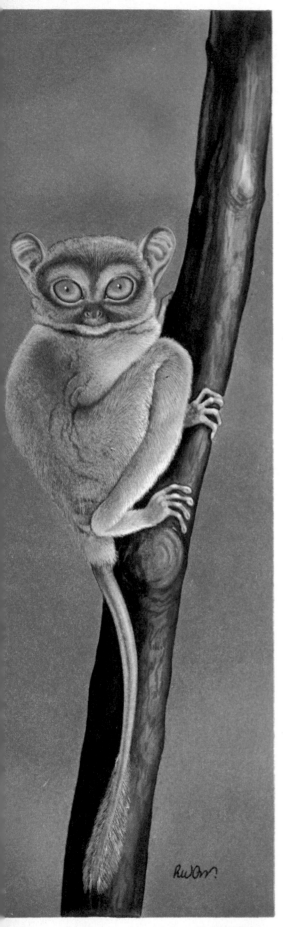

Above: Tarsier in daylight. The eyes permit very little light to enter them during the day.

Expert jumpers

The paleocene period, just over sixty million years ago, was the heyday of the Tarsiers. They colonized the earth, and what we now know as China, Europe and North America all had their representatives. But for some unknown reason Tarsiers died out in all those countries about thirty million years ago, and the only living examples of their kind now exist in the forested regions of certain islands in the south western Pacific Ocean. There is one species on the Philippine Islands, one on Celebes and one on Sumatra and Borneo (but there are also many sub-species which do not warrant being classed as separate species).

Tarsiers first became known to science when a Jesuit priest brought some back to Europe from the Pacific in the 17th century, but not until a full century later were they recognized as being like the ancestors of monkeys and apes. They are only about six inches long, but have a very long tail and peculiar "adhesive" pads on their toes that enable them to cling to smooth, upright surfaces. Their naked tails can also be pressed against any surface to stop them slipping down. Tarsiers even sleep in this manner, clinging in a hunched position to a thin, upright branch. They have flat faces, large ears and the big, staring eyes of nocturnal animals. Purely carnivorous, they stalk insects and small animals such as tree frogs, lizards and snails. Then, pouncing on their prey, they hold it firmly with both hands, closing their eyes tightly meanwhile to prevent injury from the struggling captive.

Tarsiers are usually found in the middle layers of the forest foliage and in the undergrowth. They are well-adapted for life in the trees, and can jump six feet from branch to branch, holding their limbs extended in front of them to absorb the shock of landing. Their tails are held stiffly behind them when they jump, and are flicked forward over their backs as they land. Like Bushbabies they have very long ankle bones, and this greatly increases their jumping powers. They also have what really must be the most peculiar feet and hands of all the primates – their thumbs look like fingers, being thin and long, while their fingers have large adhesive pads at their ends so that they look more like thumbs. They also have very short big toes (with even larger pads) which are set at right angles to the other toes. Two toes on each foot have nails, the others have claws.

Tarsiers are such expert jumpers and are so agile among the branches that they can often catch insects in flight – a feat that calls for a combination of good eyesight and great agility. A larger brain is necessary for this, and is one of the reasons why Tarsiers are thought to be more advanced than the primitive primates. Another reason is that they have circular nostrils that resemble our own, rather than the "twisted nostrils" of the primitive primates.

Tarsiers' large ears are moved continuously to catch every sound and, like owls, they can turn their heads completely around without moving their bodies. These techniques have helped them to survive in lands where there are many predators.

Tarsier with eyes closed ready to feed. For a long time Tarsiers were thought to be Lemurs, but later investigation resulted in their being grouped with the higher primates.

Tarsier at night. The eyes now allow as much light as possible to enter them. Notice the different appearance to the daytime eyes.

Isolated monkeys

Out on their own

THE ISLAND of Madagascar lies in the Indian Ocean not far from the eastern coast of Africa, but many years ago it was part of the mainland. It is one of the world's largest islands and is, together with a few small neighbouring islands, the only home of a number of unique animals called Lemurs.

According to palaeontologists the whole world had a large population of Lemurs about sixty million years ago. They were very primitive animals and did not develop along the same lines as other monkey-like creatures, so their homes were gradually taken over by their more advanced successors.

Fortunately for the Lemurs, however, Madagascar became separated from the African mainland before the more advanced types reached it, so Lemurs there evolved into many different species. As with other animals, many species have been replaced by others more suitable for living in each type of country – for instance, the remains of a Lemur as big as a pony have been found by fossil-seekers, but none of these has survived until recent times. There is nothing to show why this should be.

It is a great pity that, having managed to survive

Above: Mouse Lemur. Below: map of Madagascar.

for millions of years in Madagascar, Lemurs are now threatened with extinction even there. The reason for this is that forests have been felled and reed beds drained for cultivation. When animals have evolved over many years to make the most of the food and shelter provided by their habitat, they cannot suddenly adapt themselves to do without these. Because of this, several species of Lemurs are now almost extinct.

The smallest species of Lemur is the Lesser Mouse Lemur (which shares the title of smallest primate with the tiny pigmy marmoset). Its head and body measure only five inches, its tail is slightly longer and it weighs only four ounces. As it is nocturnal, little is known of its habits. It has been found asleep in holes in trees and in nests in tree tops.

These small Lemurs undergo a form of hibernation, but it has nothing to do with low temperatures; it occurs during the summer when there is a prolonged dry season, and is known as *aestivation*. During this time the Lemur rolls into a ball and sleeps in its nest or hole, drawing nourishment from semi-liquid fat stored in its tail when food was plentiful. Because of this habit Mouse Lemurs were originally thought to be a different species when caught in the summer with enlarged tails.

Dwarf Lemurs are slightly larger than Mouse Lemurs and have feet like small Bushbabies, with pads on the tips of their toes and fingers and larger pads on their palms and soles. They also undergo aestivation, and all three species are nocturnal.

The related Fork-marked Mouse Lemur is, surprisingly, a far larger animal and measures almost three feet from nose to tail tip. The most remarkable thing about this Lemur is its teeth; it actually has two pairs of canine teeth in its top jaw – a normal pair like most mammals, plus a much enlarged pair.

There are sixteen species of Lemur and some are quite large animals; the Ruffed Lemur, for instance, measures almost four feet from nose to tail tip. As it is a forest-dweller, it has suffered severely from the loss of its home and is now fairly rare. Ruffed

Above: Ruffed Lemur, which is the largest true Lemur. Below: Black Lemur.

Lemurs have long tails which help them to balance as they bounce along on their hind legs through the trees. They were once regarded as sacred animals; because of their habit of sunbathing in the early morning and late afternoon, the Malagasy people thought they were praying to the sun. These Lemurs have a bold black-and-white pattern (although this may vary, and individuals have been seen in which the white areas were almost brick-red).

Other species have equally confusing colour-schemes. In the so-called Black Lemur, for instance, the females are always pale brown with lighter underparts and have amber eyes, whereas the males are black and have orange-coloured eyes. Male and

Ringtailed Lemur. This is the best known of the Lemurs and is rather like a small, slender racoon in looks. Most Lemurs are aboreal, but the Ringtailed Lemur often lives among rocks.

female were originally thought to be different species. To confuse matters even more, both male and female young are black. Black Lemurs are tree-top dwellers, and are easily identified by the long tufts of hair that cover their ears and cheeks.

The larger and very agile Ringtailed Lemur has soft grey and white fur and a long tail alternately banded with black and white. This Lemur has scent glands, one pair of which can be seen quite clearly just above its wrists as small black hairless areas. When it is alarmed or agitated it rubs its tail on these patches and then uses it to communicate in some way with other members of the tribe. Another interesting feature of Ringtailed Lemurs is that several babies may be cared for by females other than their own mothers in a kind of nursery. Fortunately Ringtailed Lemurs have not suffered any great changes in their environment, as they live in desolate rocky places quite unsuitable for cultivation.

The related Gentle Lemurs have bare patches on their wrists similar to those of the Ringtailed Lemur, but theirs are covered with small spines. They are nocturnal, so once again little is known of their habits. It is known, however, that they have very unusual teeth, apparently specially developed for feeding on the pith of bamboos and reeds. The Snub-nosed Gentle Lemur uses its bottom front teeth, which point straight forward, as a chisel to remove the hard covering of the bamboo and reeds; it then cuts into the pith with its sharp premolar teeth, using them like scissors.

The remaining species of Lemurs – the Mongoose Lemur, the closely-related Brown Lemur and the Red-bellied Lemur – are confusingly similar in size and colour, all being varying shades of brown. But at least they are active during the daytime and so can be observed.

The unusually-named Sporting Lemurs and the Weasel Lemurs are both nocturnal species, passing the hot hours of the day in their tree nests and becoming very active at night. These Lemurs are very gregarious, and live together in large parties.

Creatures of the high forests

In the volcanic region of eastern central Madagascar the Indri lives in the high forests. The Malagasy natives call this Lemur "the dog of the forest" because of its loud dog-like cry, but the name Indri was given to it by zoologists. They mistakenly thought the natives were calling the animal by name when they said "indrizy" – which means, in fact, "there it is."

The Indri has long back legs and stands almost three feet high, with an absurd two-inch-long tail. Like the Ruffed Lemur and the Sifaka, the Indri is sacred to some tribes because it is thought to worship the sun. It is a harmless animal that feeds almost entirely on leaves, yet it is surrounded by legends. It is even credited with being able to catch spears and hurl them back at its attackers, so the natives are afraid to hunt it. The Indri is a great jumper and clings to upright branches with its large, opposable toes and fingers.

Sifakas are closely related to the Indri, and look more like a monkey than other species of Lemur. They feed mainly on flowers and leaves in the tree tops, and they too can leap from tree to tree. When descending they come down backwards. Along the sides of their bodies, between fore and hind limbs, they have a membrane which enables them to make long, gliding leaps. On the ground they keep their bodies upright and hop along holding their arms outstretched. There are two species of Sifaka, with similar thick, silky fur but confusing colour schemes; all-black and all-white forms of the Diademed Sifaka have been seen, and Verreaux's Sifaka can be many shades of brown or white.

The Woolly Indri or Avahi is a close relative of the Indri. Avahis seem to have almost circular heads because their small ears are hidden by thick fur, and their flattened faces and large, staring eyes make them look owl-like. They also have very unusual hands and feet, with large thumbs, big toes that stick out and fingers and toes of different lengths. Avahis

Aye Aye, the most remarkable of all Lemurs. The vegetable part of the Aye Aye's diet consists of the juices of sugar and bamboo plants and the meat part is supplied by wood-boring caterpillars. When finding the caterpillars the Aye Aye uses his very large ears to listen to the movements of the insects below the bark. He then gnaws away the bark with his teeth, and uses his extra-long third finger to capture his dinner.

are excellent jumpers and seldom come down to the ground. When they do they look very strange, with their arms and tails held high as they walk.

No Lemur is stranger than the Aye Aye, which was once thought to be a giant squirrel – mainly because it has two large, chisel-like teeth in its top jaw. Aye Ayes have these to feed on the pith inside the many kinds of giant bamboo that grow on the island. They also have very large ears and long middle fingers.

As the meat part of their diet is provided by wood-boring caterpillars, they listen for these inside dead trees, then hook them out with their long fingers after chiselling the wood away with their teeth. Like Tree Shrews, Aye Ayes make nests for their babies, so they are completely dependent on trees and when these are chopped down there is nowhere they can live or find food.

It is thought that there are less than one hundred Aye Ayes still living in Madagascar, so the Malagasy government has recently proclaimed the island of Nossi Mangabé a sanctuary for them. Although this island is only four miles from a large town in north-eastern Madagascar, it is still covered with the necessary forest. Several Aye Ayes have already been captured on the mainland and transferred to this sanctuary. A full-time guard of the national forest service watches over them, and there are plans afoot to transfer more Aye Ayes – and some Indris, Sifakas and Avahis too.

New World Monkeys

Bald heads and red faces

Red Uakari. These monkeys use their arms as trays to hold the food they collect.

SOUTH America is the home of many unusual primates which do not resemble those in any other region of the world. Some of these have been called half-monkeys, but this is not a very good name as it conjures up visions of animals that are half monkey and half something else. In fact, these animals are thought to be about halfway between the primitive primates and those we usually call monkeys.

The Uakaris (pronounced wah-ca-rees) are undoubtedly the most grotesque of all the monkeys. Both the white Uakari and the red Uakari look permanently emaciated and are completely bald, and to make matters worse they have vivid red faces. The White form has a long dirty-white shaggy coat, and the other a long reddish-brown coat. It was discovered by accident in an American zoo that the red colouring of their faces is only maintained if they sun themselves regularly. If they are kept in indoor cages their red faces fade to pink.

In contrast to the two "ugly mugs" the other

member of the group, the Blackheaded Uakari, is a relatively handsome monkey – very like a long-haired Spider Monkey except that it has a short tail. In fact, Uakaris have the shortest tails of all the New World monkeys; these stick out stiff and straight, yet have the same number of bones as the long tails of many other monkeys. Little is known about the habits of Uakaris in the forest, as they live high in the trees where they can benefit from the direct rays of the sun.

Saki Monkeys are close relatives of the Uakaris and although they are not so grotesque, they are certainly the most doleful-looking monkeys. Sakis also live high in the tree tops, where they eat leaves, berries and fruit. Like many arboreal animals they are not very good at walking on the ground, yet they walk with ease along branches more than one hundred feet above the forest floor.

The Hairy Saki has a cape of long hair that grows from a whorl on top of its head and covers its shoulders. Because this resembles a monk's habit, the species is often called the Monk Saki. The male White-faced Saki's face is covered with a thick mat of yellowish-white hair, but the female does not have this and in some regions has a black hairless face like the Hairy Saki. There are also two species of bearded Sakis, the Black and the White nosed; these have very soft, dense fur, similar in texture to a sheep's oily fleece, which protects them from the heavy rainfall of the tropical forests.

Within this family of South American monkeys there is one that is completely nocturnal – the only member of the higher primates with this habit. This monkey is known as the Douroucouli and as it lives like an owl, sleeping in tree holes during the day, it is not surprising that it is often called the Owl Monkey. Douroucoulis are inquisitive little animals and cannot resist peering out of their holes when they hear strange noises. This has been their undoing, because when native animal trappers tap on the trees Douroucoulis soon give away their position and are caught and shipped off to zoos or pet shops.

Squirrel Monkeys in their natural habitat.

The monkey hordes

Every year thousands of Squirrel Monkeys are exported from the jungles of South America, and in some areas they are now quite rare, particularly around human habitation. They are still, however, by far the commonest species of monkey in the New World and also the most gregarious, living in large communities that may contain over one hundred individuals. These occur mainly along the banks of the larger rivers where, in the dense growth of creepers and vines, there is more food available than in the main forest. Squirrel Monkeys venture to the ground more often than most of the South American monkeys, usually to seek food in the form of land crabs that are abroad at dusk and dawn. There have even been accounts of large troops of these monkeys raiding jungle camps to steal food.

At night Squirrel Monkeys sleep sitting on the bases of their tails; the tails themselves are wrapped around their bodies to keep them warm. Although they are said to be remarkably human in their attempts to control the younger members of the troop and keep them quiet, when they are disturbed they move rapidly off through the forest making a tremendous noise.

Squirrel Monkeys are now grouped with the prehensile-tailed species, although their long tails are only used in helping to maintain their balance. There are two species, but there are many geographical races, all differing slightly in colour. Basically, however, they are olive green and yellowish-white, with a black-tipped tail and orange feet and legs. Their tufted ears and the rings round their eyes are white, and their muzzles black. There is a considerable difference in size between males and females, the males being much larger. (There have also been reports of giant specimens being seen with the troops, but none of these has ever been photographed or caught).

Although Squirrel Monkeys live in these large troops, often in association with Capuchin Monkeys, each troop is restricted to its own territory. Large rivers form boundaries to these territories, but smaller rivers are crossed if the overhanging branches on either side are within jumping distance.

Native animal trappers catch many Squirrel Monkeys for shipment abroad by determining which is their favourite sleeping tree. They then chop down all the surrounding trees, except one which allows the monkeys access to their own tree. When the monkeys have crossed for the night the last tree is felled, leaving the monkeys' roosting tree isolated. This is then ringed with nets and the monkeys are captured without difficulty the following morning as they attempt to escape.

Squirrel Monkeys have been popular pets for many years, and they are also a favourite with seaside photographers, who dress them up and sit them on customers' shoulders. Unfortunately, although they are relatively hardy animals in their normal habitat, many Squirrel Monkeys die in the course of their journey to the pet shops. The reason for this is that these monkeys have a lot of internal parasites, usually kept in check by their free and healthy life. The shock of capture and confinement in a cage, and the loss of health through lack of the right foods combine to weaken the monkey's system so that it cannot combat the parasites.

Squirrel Monkey, showing the white rings around the eyes. These tiny monkeys are often seen in captivity.

Dwarfs of the monkey kingdom

When Spanish and Portuguese navigators first brought minute South American primates back to Europe the French named them Marmousets, meaning "of small stature." The tiny animals were popular as pets even in those days, and are said to have been carried in the large powdered wigs that were the rage at the time. Since then their name has changed slightly to Marmoset, and the group has also been divided into Marmosets and Tamarins. The two appear very similar, but Tamarins are distinguished by their longer canine teeth – a feature that has sometimes led to their being called long-tusked Marmosets. Both are highly-sensitive little animals, quite unlike any other New World primates in their behaviour – particularly in their vocabulary and facial expressions. Their high-pitched squeaks and shrill chattering are more like the noises of birds than of mammals, and some of the sounds they make are inaudible to the human ear. Seen close up, the most noticeable thing about them is that they have claws on all their digits except the big toes, which have nails. Rather than being a primitive feature, this may be a fairly recent adaptation for scampering up trees like squirrels.

All thirty-three known species of Marmosets and Tamarins live in South America, although one species also extends northwards into Central America. All the species are diurnal (seeking their food in daylight), and like Squirrel Monkeys they are gregarious and live in family groups. Most species are omnivorous and eat both plant and animal material, but a few are decidedly carnivorous and live on insects, young birds, lizards and amphibians. Babies are usually born in pairs and the proud father carries them around with him, only handing them back to the mother for feeding.

The smallest species, the Pygmy Marmoset, is also the smallest of the more advanced primates. But what these little animals lack in size is certainly made up for in temper; they seem to be unafraid of

Pigmy Marmoset, found in the upper Amazon region. This little animal is only six inches long and has a tail about seven inches long which is vaguely banded.

anything or anybody, and scream at the tops of their. voices when they think they are being threatened. They are known to exist in two widely-separated areas of South America – the north western and the south eastern tropical regions – but they may well also occur in the central forested regions. It is difficult to know for sure, as they are the most effectively camouflaged and secretive of the Marmosets.

Several species of Marmosets and Tamarins have unusual head adornments. The Geoffroy's Tamarin (the only species occurring in Central America) has the white hair on top of its head styled in Mohican Indian fashion, while the related Cotton-top Tamarin's hair style is even more bizarre – it has long, flowing white plumes reminiscent of a Zulu warrior. The so-called Common Marmoset is often confused with two other closely-related ones, but the true Common species has white ear-tufts, whereas

Below, left: Geoffrey's Tamarin, which lives in Panama. This animal has an odd arrangement of teeth, as its lower incisors are very short leaving the canines projecting above the tooth row. Right: Black-plumed Marmoset.

JANE BURTON

Map showing the location of Marmosets in South America.

the White-eared Marmoset has white ear-plumes and the similar Black-pencilled Marmoset has black ear-plumes. The Emperor Tamarin has a drooping moustache so long that it hangs down on to its arms, but this does not seem to interfere with any of the animal's daily tasks.

The most noticeable characteristic of the Red-handed Tamarin, which lives in the northern forests of South America, is its hands and feet, which look just as if they had been dipped in bright orange paint. Like the bald-headed Uakaris there are also bald-headed Tamarins, and the Pied Tamarin is a member of this group. It has a black face and ears, long silky white fur and a black-and-white tail. The related Martin's Tamarin is purple-brown in colour with contrasting white-furred hands and feet, and dark blue spots on its ears. Another strangely-marked species is the Silver Marmoset, which has long silky white fur on its body and a black tail, so that in dim light it appears to be tail-less. This Marmoset has a pink face, large naked ears, and a bald head covered with blotches that at first glance look rather like sores.

The most unusual species of the entire group is the Golden Lion Marmoset, which is the most highly-coloured of all the primates. This Marmoset is a deep golden yellow, with a naked face of the same colour. The first one to reach Europe alive is said to have been owned by Madame Pompadour. Unfortunately, the intense glowing colour of most individuals of this species fades and becomes very drab when they are kept in captivity. Like the males of the other species, the Golden Lion Marmoset is a good father, and is even said to act as midwife when his babies are born. This Marmoset has two closely-related species in the south eastern Brazilian forests – the Golden-headed Tamarin, which is basically black with a golden-yellow mane and some yellow on its tail, and the Golden-rumped Tamarin, which is also black but has a bright golden-yellow tail, fore-arms, hands and feet. These three species have been placed in a separate group from the others as

H. E. UIBLE

they are considered to fit in somewhere between the true Marmosets and the Tamarins.

Although they are not members of the same family as the Marmosets and Tamarins, the Titi Monkey and Goeldi's Monkey are also rather small species and deserve to be included here. Goeldi's Monkey (or Callimico) is a very rare animal, about twice the size of the Golden Lion Marmoset. It is clothed in silky, jet-black hair that is extra long on the head and shoulders. At one time the curious suggestion was made that this monkey was more closely related to the Marmosets than to any other primates because of its parasites. It is certainly true that some parasites are what is called host specific – that is, they are only to be found on certain closely-related animals. However, it has been discovered quite recently that the Callimico mother carries her babies, which places this species closer to the Capuchins than to the Marmosets, where the males act as nurse-maids. The Titis are similar-sized monkeys, of which the Necklaced Titi is the most spectacular. This is clad in lustrous copper-coloured fur, with black limbs, tail and ears contrasting sharply with white face and hands.

Pygmy Marmoset, joint smallest of all primates along with the Lesser Mouse Lemur.

White-faced Capuchin. Capuchins are a large family of tropical American monkeys, whose name comes from the thick hair on the crown of their heads, resembling the cowl of a Capuchin Monk. These monkeys are very intelligent and have a highly developed brain. They do well in captivity and have been known to survive in zoos for 25 years.

Typical monkeys

Five-handed monkeys

IN AFRICA and Asia several species of monkeys live on the ground and seldom climb trees, but in the whole of the Central and South American tropics all the monkeys are tree climbers and hardly ever set foot on the ground. All the primates of this area, apart from those already mentioned, have prehensile tails with which they cling to branches, leaving their hands and feet free for other tasks. These prehensile or "hand-tailed" monkeys are in fact the only primates in the world to have this extra "hand", although there are other mammals that can cling to branches with their tails – Opossums, Kinkajous and Tree Porcupines, for example. Most people consider "five-handed" monkeys to be typical monkeys, but in fact it is an uncommon trait. Only eighteen species, out of the total world primate population of almost two hundred species, can hang by their tails.

The commonest prehensile-tailed monkeys are the Capuchins, which are widespread throughout the canopy forests from southern Mexico to northern Argentina. As the forests they inhabit vary from humid lowland rain forests to the cooler mountain forests of the Andean slopes they have considerable colour variation, and sometimes what would appear to be an overlapping and interbreeding of species.

Basically, however, there are two types of Capuchins, with two species of each type. The two species of the first type are the small White-throated Capuchins of Central America and the Cinnamon Capuchins of the Amazon forests — both of which are agile and mischievous, though often very nervous, little animals. The Central American species has a white face, chest, shoulders and upper arms, and the rest of its body is black. The Cinnamon Capuchins vary from pale fawn to a kind of dark

Map showing the location of Capuchins in South America.

gingery-brown colour. Capuchins of the second type are only slightly larger, but are frequently moody and aggressive animals. Both species in this group are dark brown with darker limbs and tail, the Weeper Capuchin having a black cap and, occasionally, pronounced ear-tufts. This gives it a horned appearance very similar to the other species – the Horned or Tufted Capuchin – which has high tufts above its ears and heavy sideburns. Earlier this century Weeper Capuchins were the favourites of organ grinders, who trained them to doff their little caps and collect money from the audience.

Capuchins have always been considered more intelligent than other monkeys, and are especially interesting to zoologists because they have convoluted brains similar to those of human beings. Some years ago a German scientist carried out extensive experimental work over a long period with Capuchin Monkeys, and his main conclusion was that they exceeded even the apes in some of their abilities, particularly in the use of "tools." One Capuchin Monkey, given tools that were completely new to it, used a piece of wire to secure a special stick, with which it could reach an even longer stick to bring food within its reach – all inside a few minutes. In about three minutes, another learned how to use a live rat attached to string to gather food that had been placed out of reach. Capuchins have also made drawings and paintings, and are the only monkeys to have done this.

In zoological gardens, Capuchins have proved to be one of the hardiest and most adaptable species. When tropical monkeys are brought to zoos in the British Isles and other northern countries it is necessary to acclimatize them, otherwise they would catch cold and probably develop pneumonia in outdoor cages. If they are allowed to accustom themselves slowly to a northern climate, many kinds of monkeys become very hardy and even play out in the snow. African and Asian monkeys are generally best at withstanding cold weather, but Capuchins are surprisingly hardy too. When I was in charge of the animals in a large zoo some years ago we had an old Weeper Capuchin called Cheeta, who shared a cage with his friend Spi, a large Spider Monkey. Capuchins often live for thirty years or more, by which time they have lost most of their teeth, may be almost bald and are usually very irritable. Cheeta was no exception, but he was also a very intelligent monkey. One bitterly cold afternoon in midwinter, he managed to release the catch on his cage door and immediately climbed some tall trees near the zoo entrance. On this occasion Spi showed more sense, and stayed in the cage where he had access to his heated den. Not even the most exotic fruits would entice Cheeta down, but later that day, under cover of darkness and a freezing fog, he came down and dashed off to another hiding-place. We thought he had little chance of surviving, but, to our amazement he was discovered the following morning, fit and well, fast asleep on the seat of a dodgem car in the nearby amusement park. He had sensibly slipped beneath the heavy tarpaulin cover, and this had protected him from the frost.

Capuchins' tails are not as highly-specialized for hanging by as those of the Howler, Spider and Woolly Monkeys, but they are still very useful for gathering food, and there have been instances of their using them to throw objects. A Capuchin I once knew in a South American zoo was kept chained to a platform of his own, out of reach of visitors. Whenever this monkey took exception to a visitor – which was frequently, as he was a grumpy old chap – he broke twigs off nearby branches and threw these, and sometimes his fruit too.

In their natural habitat Capuchins live in groups of about three dozen individuals. They are completely omnivorous, eating practically anything animal or vegetable they can find. They venture down to the forest floor rather more often than the other prehensile-tailed species, usually to raid crops planted in clearings by Indian tribes. Some of these tribes still eat monkeys, shooting them with shotguns, bows and arrows or blowpipes.

Baby Capuchin, who lives within a large group. Capuchins are highly sociable and vivacious animals.

Twenty-four-hour choristers

Before I visited the South American jungle I read many accounts of Howler Monkeys and the noise they make, but I was totally unprepared for the volume or type of sound they produce. I expected to hear a howling like that of wolves, or the wind, so the first time I heard a deep, roaring noise I did not at once associate it with Howlers.

These monkeys have greatly enlarged throats and lower jaws, and modified bony structures lying more or less where our tongues do. These are connected with the throat and act as sound boxes to increase the volume of the noise, which really is tremendous. Howlers live in small troops and roaring is a means of staking their claim on a territory; it also informs one troop of the existence and whereabouts of another. Usually the dominant male starts howling first, and is then joined by the other adults in the

Howler Monkey. This is the largest of the New World monkeys, being about the size of a small dog. Howlers have extraordinary vocal powers, and their roar can be heard for several miles. They are not very intelligent and have small under-developed brains, perhaps proving the old saying that empty vessels make the most noise. The Indians have been able to tame most of the Brazilian forest monkeys, but even they have had no success with Howlers.

troop. Where the territory is small, there is obviously more frequent howling to prevent trespassing, and this goes on day and night.

It is not always necessary to venture into the depths of the jungle to hear Howlers. On Trinidad, for instance, a troop of Howler Monkeys lives on a small hill not far from one of the island's main beaches. It is a heavily-forested territory, separated from similar areas to the north by cultivated land and to the south by a large freshwater swamp. Obviously this territory is hardly likely to be invaded by other Howler Monkeys, yet the troop in possession still roars regularly.

The Trinidad species referred to is the Red Howler Monkey, which has a thick coat of reddish-brown fur. In Central America there is an all-black species, and in the Brazilian forests there is a black one with red feet and hands. All these species use their prehensile tails to the fullest advantage, and even swing by them to reach food that would otherwise be out of reach. They are the leaf-eaters of the New World, although they also eat fruit and berries. When adult, Howlers are almost always morose, solemn animals, and when mature individuals have been captured for zoos they have seldom thrived because of their temperament. Baby Howlers are completely different, although they are not as playful as the young of other species of monkeys. They often become so dependent on their foster-parents when they are being bottle-reared that they cannot bear to lose sight of them for a second – which can be rather trying at times!

Howlers have a peculiar way of moving through the tree tops (running, rather than climbing), but they can move very quickly when necessary. They seldom venture below the upper canopy of the forest, which means they are at the mercy of the giant Harpy Eagles and Crested Eagles that fly high above the tree tops searching for monkeys and sloths, their favourite food. Even if a Howler does drop down through the foliage, there is little chance of his escaping a really determined Harpy Eagle.

Spider Monkeys are the most highly-specialized of the "hand-tailed" monkeys, and have elongated limbs for swinging beneath the branches. Their hands merely hook on to each branch rather than gripping it firmly, and consequently, their thumbs have been of so little use to them that over the years they have been lost altogether. These monkeys use the swinging motion of their bodies to carry them forward to the next branch, rather like circus trapeze artists. This way of travelling is called *brachiation,* and is similar to that used by the Gibbons of south-east Asia. Spider Monkeys' long, thick muscular tails can support the weight of their bodies for a considerable time; this is no mean feat, as the adults are quite large animals and develop enormous pot-bellies as they mature. Wild Spider Monkeys have been known to use their tails to throw sticks at passers-by.

Geoffroy's Spider Monkey of Central America is a very common species, with reddish-brown hair and lighter colouring on its chest and beneath its arms and legs. In northern South America there is an extra-large species with long black hair and gaunt, bright-red features. The larger Woolly Spider Monkey occurs in a rather small area of south eastern

Woolly Monkey. This has very soft fur and a naked black face that looks almost human. Its fur resembles that of a hare, and in fact its generic name Lagothrix means "hare-hair".

Brazil. It is a rare animal, half-way between a Spider Monkey and a Woolly Monkey, and little is known of its habits. Its colour varies from grey to yellowish-brown and it may reach a length of five feet from head to tip of tail.

Woolly Monkeys have long had the reputation of being good pets, but this is completely unjustifiable. As babies they are gentle and make excellent companions, but as they mature they become sullen and liable to attack their owners without warning. As they have extremely powerful jaws and long canine teeth, and attack with a sort of controlled frenzy, their victims may be seriously injured. Like Spider Monkeys, they develop pot-bellies when they mature and in Brazil are known by the un-complimentary name of *barrigudos*, or "bag-bellies". They live in small groups – often in association with Spider, Capuchin and Howler Monkeys – without any signs of hostility or squabbling.

Woolly Monkeys have short, dense coats and close-cropped heads that look almost as if they have had a crew cut. There are only three recognized species; the Smokey, which is grey or brownish-black with a darker head; the Humboldt's, which is pale chocolate-brown all over; and the very rare Hendee's Woolly Monkey, which is a rich reddish-brown with a buff patch around its nose.

Above: Red-faced Spider Monkey. Left: Variegated Spider Monkey. The Spider Monkey is closely related to the Woolly Monkey, but its fur is coarser in texture.

African long-tailed monkeys

Moustaches and spot-noses

THE VAST tropical forest zone of Africa extends from Sierra Leone on the Atlantic coast, through the Congo almost to Uganda. It is the home of many species of very long-tailed monkeys, most of which are known as Guenons. These monkeys are highly-adapted for life in the tree tops, and can probably move faster through them than a man can walk below. Also, their young seem to mature more quickly than the young of many other monkeys and can follow their parents along the branches at a very early age. Most species are highly-coloured and have unusual facial markings. In the thick foliage of the closed canopy forests bright patches, spots, stripes, and colourful beards help them to communicate with each other (whereas primates less dependent on trees, such as Baboons and Macaques, have developed facial expressions and grimacing as a means of signalling).

Spot-nosed and Moustached Monkeys are amongst the most bizarre of the long-tailed monkeys. The former (also called the White-nosed and the Putty-

De Brazza's Monkey, which is the largest of the Guenons and is found from the Cameroons to southern Congo. Unlike most of its relatives this monkey takes readily to water though it mostly lives in trees.

nosed Monkey) is common in the West African forests, and has several sub-species or races that differ slightly in basic colour and in the extent of the white nose spot. The Spot-nosed Monkey is a small, intelligent animal, dark olive green in colour and with a blackish face. On its nose is an inverted heart-shaped spot composed of short, stiff white hairs. Some have reddish areas on their chests but these have been found to wash out with hot soapy water, and are thought to be caused by vegetable dyes. The Moustached Guenons are similar in basic colouration but have bright blue faces and pure white moustaches, plus golden cheek-tufts. Both species live in large bands in the tree tops, where they feed on fruit, leaves, berries and small animals such as tree frogs and snails.

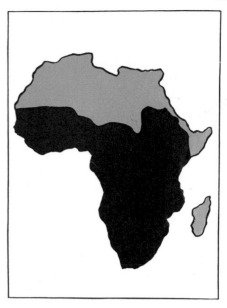

Map showing location of Guenons in Africa.

Another species with a pronounced moustache is the rare Allen's Swamp Monkey, a greenish-black animal with a yellow chest and throat and a broad black moustache that tapers almost to its ears. It was only discovered early this century, in the swampy forests of the north western Congo region that are flooded during the rainy season. As far as we know these monkeys do not swim and never intentionally enter the water of the swamps. They are so unlike the Guenons that they have been placed in a separate group, and this also applies to the smallest species of these long-tailed monkeys, the tiny Talapoin Monkey. Many scientists classify it separately because its teeth are different from those of other Guenons, and because it has very short fingers that are partially webbed. Other zoologists, however, think differently and call it the Pygmy Guenon.

The largest and most strikingly-marked Guenon is De Brazza's Monkey, which has a conspicuous white beard. This Guenon is generally greenish-black, with darker limbs that are white on the inside. Above the eyes there is a whitish brow patch, separated from the black fur of the crown by a narrow strip of white. De Brazza's Monkey is thought to represent the most advanced type of Guenon, having developed its elaborate markings to the peak of perfection. It lives in the central African forests, in the Congo and in Uganda.

There are two other conspicuously-bearded species, the Diana Monkey and the closely-related Roloway Monkey. Forest tribes still hunt these monkeys for food, as they have done for thousands of years, but professional hunters who seek them for selling in the local markets are now threatening their continued existence. These two species have been described as the most handsome of the Guenons, even though they lack the brilliant colours of some of the other species. They are boldly marked with glossy bluish-black tinged with brown on their upper-parts, and have contrasting pure white under-parts. The main difference between the two is that the Diana has a stubby black beard and the Roloway a longer white one. Both make excellent pets when young, but like all Guenons, they are very strong-willed when mature and resent being controlled by man.

Guenons in general are impressive leapers, and run along branches to the outermost edges of the trees before jumping off. They do not seem to aim at any particular branch, but land with a great crash in the foliage and quickly vanish into it. The commonest arboreal species is the Mona Monkey, which has a wide distribution throughout practically the whole forest zone. Typical of the Guenons, it walks along branches on all fours, gripping firmly with its opposable thumbs and big toes and keeping its balance with the help of its long tail. It eats practically anything edible in the way of vegetable and animal foods, and is particularly fond of insects and tree snails. Monas lack the unique facial adornments of other Guenons but are still striking monkeys when adult, their yellowish-white under-parts contrasting with the darker fur above, which is relieved with white rump patches and yellow cheek tufts. They live in large, noisy troops and reach maturity at about five years of age.

Crowned Guenons are so closely allied to Mona Monkeys that some zoologists prefer to call them sub-species of the Monas, even though they are quite dissimilar in colouring. There are three races of these monkeys, all with green backs, bright yellow stomachs and chests and crowns of backward-pointing hair. Among the most highly-coloured of all the primates, their greens and yellows appear vivid and fresh compared with the dull olives and faded yellows of other species. One race has three black lines running upwards from its eyes. Below these are thick, yellow back-swept side-whiskers and, to enhance its appearance even more, this monkey also has a yellow chin and upper lip.

Spot-nosed Guenon, which is easily distinguishable from its relatives by the white spot on the end of its nose. Guenons, like Macaques, have cheek pouches and live mostly in the trees feeding on fruit, leaves and insects.

JANE BURTON

Hussars of the savannahs

By no means all Guenons are arboreal, and many live in the open grasslands which extend to the north, east and south of the great forests. These grasslands act as intermediate zones between forests (where the rainfall is very high) and deserts (where it rains only at long intervals of three to four years, but then very heavily). In most places the grasslands are dotted with trees, and where these are plentiful the country is known as savannah woodland.

Grasslands are the home of hordes of Grass Monkeys and Patas (or Hussar) Monkeys, which are respectively semi-terrestrial and almost completely terrestrial. Between these ground-dwellers and the full-time tree-dwellers, however, there is another group known as the Diadem Monkeys, of which there are about twenty recognized races. Some of these inhabit the edges of the forests, while others live in more open woodland, especially the gallery forests which follow the rivers right into the heart of the grasslands. The races are all very similar (otherwise they would be separated into different species), with greenish-black coats, whitish marking about their faces in the form of collars and whiskers, and often a distinct diadem around their heads. They spend much of their time on the ground, searching for insects, seeds and berries, and in some areas they live in almost semi-arid scrubland. Unlike their tree-living relatives they are not restricted to the closed canopy forests and therefore have a wider range both to the north and south. Some races occur in South Africa, the best-known of these being the Samango Monkey, which lives in Natal and Zululand.

The commonest monkeys in South Africa, and in fact throughout the grasslands, are the three races of Grass Monkeys. Their basic colour is yellowish-green, often tinged with blue or brown, and they have a black face with a white surrounding fringe. The Vervet Monkey, which is the South African

Patas monkey from Sudan. This monkey is also known as the Hussar Monkey, because of its soldierly bearing.

race, has darker hands and feet and is reddish beneath the tail. These monkeys are pests in the farmlands, and raid crops whenever these are left unguarded. It is even suspected that they sit and wait patiently in nearby trees until the watchman leaves or falls asleep, whereupon they promptly dash down to feed.

Grass Monkeys spend the hours of darkness in trees, where they are relatively safe from predators, and during the day they wander about in large groups searching for insects, small lizards, seeds and roots. They also climb trees to feed on shoots, leaves, nuts, fruit and seeds. They do not appear to be as strictly territorial as the tree-living Guenons and range over quite large regions, returning to each area after several months' wandering. These monkeys are common in zoos, where the race most frequently seen is the Green Monkey (the one from West Africa) which is far more greenish in body colouring than the others.

In East Africa the common race of Grass Monkey is known as the Grivet Monkey; this differs from the others in having long white tufts on the sides of its face. Grivet Monkeys have played an important part in laboratory research. They are often caught by means of large nets, attached to rockets that are fired over the trees in which they have taken refuge, and in this way several hundreds can be captured at one time for the world's research establishments. In fact, so many have been exported from East Africa that some countries there have found it necessary to ban their export, or at least to restrict the numbers exported, until the populations have recovered. As well as the danger of extermination, the authorities have to consider the effects that over-trapping may have on the balance of nature. Leopards, for instance, eat large numbers of these monkeys and would have to find alternative food. They would probably take to raiding farms and killing domestic animals such as goats or calves. Every animal has a part to play in maintaining this balance, and when we interfere it has serious consequences and causes

Map showing location of Patas Monkeys in Africa.

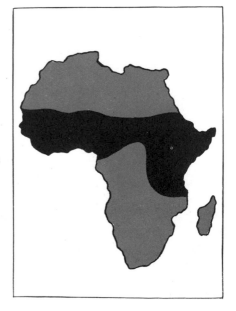

upsets that are not easily put right.

These semi-arboreal Guenons are not the only monkeys in the African savannahs. There are others that spend practically all their lives on the ground and seldom venture into the trees, and being quite different from the Guenons these have been placed in a group of their own. Once again there are several races, but they are all commonly known as Patas Monkeys or Nisnas Monkeys. They do not extend as far south as the Grass Monkeys – Tanzania in East Africa being the limit of their range – and they live in far drier regions than any of the species we have mentioned so far. Like many animals of waterless areas, their body colouring is sandy-orange to match the general colour of their surroundings and they have become adapted for surviving without having to drink regularly. They are adapted also for running, rather than climbing, and have long limbs and plantigrade feet and hands – in other words, they walk on the whole, flat surface of each, as we walk on our feet.

The race known as the Nisnas Monkey occurs in the eastern grasslands and has a white nose, whereas the others, including the well-known Patas Monkey of the western grasslands, have black noses. Collectively they are often referred to as Soldier, Military or Hussar Monkeys, because of their military bearing and marching habits, and their reddish coats which resemble the uniforms of hussar regiments. Also, they have the habit of leaving "sentries" posted on elevated outposts when they feel threatened. They live in large groups which, like the Grass Monkeys, travel over a wide area, searching the ground for small animal life and vegetable matter. When they are alarmed they sometimes jump up and down excitedly on the same spot, and it is thought that this strange behaviour may originally have resulted from jumping in long grass to get a better view of the surroundings. These monkeys also have a strange jaw formation reminiscent of those other larger ground-dwellers, the Mangabeys and Macaques.

Vervet Monkey, of South Africa. This animal plays an important part in laboraory research. Its face is sooty black and is surrounded by a white band.

Green Monkey, or Tantalus Guenon, playfully hiding behind a leaf. This monkey's fur is a mixture of black and yellow, giving a green effect. It is found in west Africa.

JANE BURTON

The dog monkeys

Scoundrels of the monkey kingdom

MACAQUES, Mangabeys and Baboons swarm in their thousands in every type of habitat – in the swamps, the grasslands and the forests, on hillsides and even on the highest mountains. Macaques, with the exception of the Barbary Ape, live in Asia and Mangabeys in Africa. Baboons also live in Africa and in some parts of Arabia. They are all related, however, and are unlike many of the other primates in that it is possible to tell their sex from a distance, the male being normally far larger than the female and often having exaggerated ornaments. Both sexes have large cheek pouches in which they stuff food to eat at their leisure. A noticeable feature of the female is the large pink or red swelling that grows at certain times of the year at the base of the tail. This is perfectly normal and denotes that the owner is mature, healthy and able to breed.

The young of most of them are agile, playful and mischievous, whereas the mature animals are untrustworthy, moody, aggressive and armed with a fearsome set of teeth. They "yawn" frequently, but this is a deliberate action designed to intimidate and show off their teeth. On their own they are cowards, but in a large enough group they will tackle any adversary without fear.

They really are the scoundrels of the whole monkey kingdom – tough, adaptable and destructive. They are all gregarious in their habits, and live in troops controlled by a dominant male. Troops of Baboons, including Mandrills and Drills, (which are special kinds of Baboons) are particularly troublesome. They are sometimes aggressive even towards human beings, and there are reports of their having killed people who had wandered alone into their territory. Even leopards seldom risk the fury of a troop, and prefer to attack isolated individuals.

Long-tailed Macaque sitting on a plantation fence. Macaques are heavily-built and there is a variation in the length of their tails.

R. K. MURTON

Above: Baboons, one with young. These ground-living, long-muzzled monkeys grow to a height of four feet. They live in barren, rocky districts in large troops which are very fierce and dangerous if approached.

The best known of them all is probably the Rhesus Macaque; not only has it given its name to a particular blood group, it is also the kind of monkey most frequently seen in zoos. No matter how small the zoo, if there are monkeys on exhibition they will almost certainly be Rhesus Macaques. They are one of the medium-tailed species and, when mature at six years of age, are stocky and often obese, weighing about twenty pounds. They live mainly in forested regions of south eastern Asia, but in parts of India where their territory has been taken over for cultivation they have been driven into the towns. There they are said to live like rats, scavenging for scraps and raiding the rubbish dumps. They are known as Bandars in India, and in districts where they are regarded as sacred they are allowed to steal the crops and ransack the temples without fear of reprisal.

The largest species of Macaque has the odd description of Pig-tailed, yet its small tail is not as pig-like as the absurdly tiny, naked, curly tail of the Stump-tailed Macaque. Tame Pig-tailed Macaques have been trained to assist their owners in collecting coconuts and other fruit, and recently they have also assisted the Forestry Department in Malaya by collecting botanical specimens from the tops of tall trees. Adult male Pigtails are large, powerful animals, more than a match for any unarmed man, so only females or young are used for this work.

RUSS KINNE

Rhesus Monkeys, which are the best-known of all monkeys and almost bound to be found in any zoo, no matter how small. Natives of India, these monkeys have long brown fur all over except for a naked area on the buttocks.

When collecting specimens or picking coconuts they have belts around their waists with leads attached, and are controlled from the ground by shouted directions.

The Stumptailed or Red-faced Macaques are also large and powerful monkeys, rivalling the Pigtails in size and aggressiveness. These monkeys occur in northern regions, where they live on the mountainsides and have much denser coats and unmistakable red faces. Little is known of their behaviour in the wild but the opposite is the case where their relatives, the Japanese Macaques, are concerned. Some years ago, studies were made of the types of food that Japanese Macaques eat, and it was discovered that they ate over one hundred different types, although each troop had its own particular food preference. For instance, some raided paddy fields, yet others living near rice-growing areas never did. Some had the habit of washing the sweet potatoes they stole from the fields before eating them, and others ate them unwashed. It was found that when one monkey in a troop started doing something different, the habit was picked up by the other members and passed on to the babies. It was also found that when an adult male, especially the dominant male of a troop, started new feeding habits, these spread more quickly than when animals lower down the social scale – females, young males, etc. – started them.

Like the Japanese Macaque, the Lion-tailed species of the hill forests of southern India is also a rare animal. Usually shy and retiring, it is aggressive enough on occasions to have attacked human beings and even to have killed children. These animals are undoubtedly powerful when mature, and their enormous canine teeth would not look out of place in a leopard's jaw. Their tails resemble a lion's tail, and they have a large ruff of grey hair around their faces.

Two species of Macaques are commonly called apes because they are tail-less. The most famous of these is the Barbary Ape that lives on the Rock of

Gibraltar. According to legend, Great Britain will only rule the Rock as long as the Barbary Ape remains there. This ape occurs in the wild state in North Africa, and it is almost certain that it was introduced to the Rock by man – possibly by the Romans or the Moors. The other species, the Black Ape, is a native of the island of Celebes in Indonesia. It is jet black and has an unusual crest of stiff hairs on its head.

Zoologists include a number of large, long-tailed monkeys in the same group as Macaques and Baboons. These are the Mangabeys, which live in the forests of tropical Africa and are totally arboreal. They are rather unlike their relatives, in behaviour at least, as they do not show either the self-assurance of the Macaques nor the aggressiveness of the Baboons. Crested Mangabeys are striking animals that have crests of black hair spreading out behind their heads. The commoner Sooty Mangabeys are a greyish-black colour, but there are several races, and one – the Red-capped Mangabey – has a white neck and a reddish-brown crown. They all have exaggerated cheek whiskers, sweeping upwards away from their faces. Their white upper eyelids are visible even in the gloom of the forests, and with these and their blinking and grimacing signals they were able to communicate with each other without uttering a sound – most unusual for monkeys!

The largest of the Baboons are the Mandrills and the Drills, and these stocky, well-muscled animals are also the largest primates after the Great Apes. They are dog-like in appearance, with short tails, and when sitting they are almost three feet high. Adult Mandrills are brown with yellowish under-parts and have tufts of yellow hair on the sides of their heads, but their most unusual features are the highly-coloured areas of skin on their faces and hindquarters. Their noses are bright red and the ridged skin on either side is blue, while their hind-quarters are shades of red and blue which blend to produce mauve in places. Their whiskers are pure

Barbary Ape and 13-day-old baby, at Chessington Zoo. The Barbary Ape is native to North Africa and the Rock of Gibralter, and is unusual in having practically no tail.

white. It takes about eight years for a baby Mandrill to attain its full size and glory.

Mandrills live in the forests of West Africa, but spend most of their time on the ground searching for food. Mature males have teeth as large as those of the biggest leopards and a troop can easily deal with any such animal foolish enough to attack it in the open. Drills are a little smaller, with black faces, high cheekbones and heavily-ridged areas at the sides of the nose. They are just as aggressive and dangerous as Mandrills, however, and equally able to defend themselves. Both species are actually very specialized forest forms of Baboon.

The true Baboons are also restricted to Africa (plus a small area of southern Arabia) and live mainly in the grasslands, savannah and dry rocky regions. Where parts of their range have been cultivated they have taken to the neighbouring hills, and periodically raid the crops in the valleys.

Baboons are all very much alike in shape and behaviour. They live in large groups and walk around on all fours like dogs, with their tails held high and bent in the middle. They eat roots, seeds, shoots and other vegetable matter, and whatever they can find in the way of small animal life. There have even been instances of Baboons eating small monkeys, and in South Africa farmers are occasionally troubled by Baboons killing their sheep and goats.

The most familiar of the Baboons are probably those known as the Hamadryas or Sacred Baboons, which live in north eastern Africa and neighbouring parts of the Arabian peninsula. Years ago they also occurred in the Nile Valley, and in ancient Egypt they were sacred, as they were believed to be direct descendants of the gods; when they died they were embalmed and buried in a sitting position. In the Valley of Kings near Thebes a large monkey cemetery has been unearthed, and examination of the bones has revealed that the animals undoubtedly suffered from malnutrition and were kept in cages too small for them. In the same period they were also

Each troop of Baboons is a family unit, and its members never wander far from one another. When a troop is ranging its area in search of food a definite grouping can be seen, with young juveniles, females carrying babies and dominant males all in the middle. In front and in the rear go other females and young males. Baboons tend to gather round any female with a newborn infant, just as human beings stop to admire a new baby.

trained to sweep the temples and turn the irrigation wheels to water the fields.

Gelada Baboons are slightly larger and also live in Ethiopia, but are restricted to the slopes of the highest mountains. Like the Hamadryas they have a cape of long hair hanging from their shoulders, but a characteristic peculiarly their own is the red patch on their chests, which at certain times of the year has small swellings linked across it almost like a necklace. These Baboons have a gaunt appearance, and their hollow cheeks accentuate their large bulbous muzzles and the ridges between their nostrils and eyes. There are few trees in high altitude areas for the Gelada Baboons to climb, so when settling for the night they seek inaccessible ledges where they will be relatively safe from prowling leopards.

The capable swimmers

Man's nearest primate relatives, the apes, cannot swim instinctively and there seems to be no record of their ever having been taught. They have as much fear of falling into deep water as non-swimming humans and yet, like children, the Great Apes will often wade into shallow water and enjoy splashing about. Many monkeys can swim when necessary; several species of Guenons, for example, have been seen to drop into crocodile-infested rivers when they were being pursued and there was no other avenue of escape. Within one family of primates, however – the Macaques and Baboons – there are several species that swim regularly. These monkeys appear to swim instinctively, like dogs, and those that I myself have seen swimming used a stroke that might well be described as a "monkey dog-paddle". Their forelimbs, bent at the elbow, were moved up and down alternately in the water, and their legs trailed behind them.

The versatile Rhesus Macaques are particularly good swimmers, and are among the few monkeys that appear to swim deliberately merely for the fun of it. I have often watched young ones swimming across the large pool in their zoo enclosure on very warm days, when it would have been far easier and certainly much less energetic to have walked around the edge. Some years ago a number of Rhesus Macaques were introduced on to an island in the West Indies. It was hoped that they would settle down and multiply there and save North American research laboratories the trouble of bringing them all the way from southern Asia. However, the monkeys were determined not to stay on the island, and two of them actually succeeded in crossing the half mile of water between it and the mainland, It is, of course, just possible that they hitched a lift on some driftwood, but they may well have swum the whole distance as others were still swimming strongly when picked out of the sea a quarter of a mile from the island.

Crab-eating Macaque of India, which lives near the sea and its estuaries or inland rivers, eating the crustacea found there. This Macaque has a long tail but lacks a mane.

Below, left and right: Rhesus Macaque, which is, like De Brazza's Guenon, one of the few monkeys that appear to swim just for the fun of it.

In zoos these swimming monkeys are often kept in large open enclosures, surrounded by a water barrier and a smooth wall with an overhang. The water is too deep to allow the monkeys to stand at the base of the wall, so they cannot leap over it but are forced to keep on swimming or sink.

Other Macaques could almost be said to swim for their living, as they feed mainly on water creatures. These are the Crab-eating Macaques, which have a wide distribution throughout south east Asia and the Indonesian islands. They live in lowland areas and are never found far from water. Most of their numbers live along the coasts, on the tidal mudflats, and in estuaries, creeks and mangrove swamps, where they feed on crabs and other crustaceans. There is little else for them to eat in any case, even in the mangrove swamps. They are thought to be a late addition to the monkeys of that area, forced to make do with any habitat that was unoccupied. To survive they had to eat crabs, and so of necessity developed into the monkey kingdom's most expert swimmers. Those of the Crab-eaters that live inland along the river banks have the more usual omnivorous monkey diet of fruit, seeds, leaves and small animal life. Another species of Macaque, which lives only on the island of Formosa, is also a beachcomber and swims regularly.

RUSS KINNE

JANE BURTON

Snow monkeys

Japanese Macaques, which live farther north than any other primate except man. These short-tailed monkeys are found only on the Japanese Islands.

In Russia a few years ago a number of Rhesus Macaques were kept in an outdoor cage without any heat throughout two winters, The temperature was below freezing point most of the time, and on several occasions there were thirty degrees of frost. These tropical monkeys were imported from southern Asia, where they had been accustomed to a temperature of about twenty seven degrees Centigrade – rather like a very good English summer all the year round. Yet they were able to acclimatize themselves to temperatures at least a hundred degrees below this, and what is more they suffered no ill effects from this exposure to "arctic" conditions. Naturally this was accomplished very gradually as no animal can accustom itself to such extreme temperatures in a short period. By the time these Rhesus Macaques were used to living outside in the cold they had developed thick, glossy coats, had good appetites and were generally in much better condition than others of the same species kept in heated cages.

Rhesus Macaques are, of course, noted for their adaptability, but there are other species within the Macaque and Baboon families that are just as hardy, and in fact habitually live in regions where winters are harsh and food is very scarce. It is normal to associate monkeys with the tropics (which is, of course, where most of them live), but several species do live in temperate regions where conditions in winter would be more suitable for Polar Bears. Some of the Stump-tailed Macaques live in the high central areas of China, in the provinces of Sikiang and Sze-Chwan, where snow covers the ground in winter. These Macaques are rugged animals that grow thick winter coats. When they are very cold, their normal bright red faces change to blue.

A related species, the Japanese Macaque, has the most northerly range of the non-human primates. On the island of Honshu these animals are often forced to dig into the snow to find sufficient food as, apart from moss and the bark of trees, there is really very little to sustain them during the winter; neither is there any shelter for them, as most of the trees lose their leaves in the autumn. The monkeys have to seek protection from the snow-laden winds by huddling in rock crevices or pressing against the boles of large trees. It is different for the babies, who are assured of a regular supply of warm milk and have their mothers' thick winter coats to snuggle into. For them it is a time of great fun, and they revel in the snow.

The only Macaque found in Africa – the Barbary Ape – also has to be a hardy animal as it lives high in the mountains of North Africa. During the winter it survives on bark, pine cones, roots and whatever else it can glean from the bleak landscape.

It was discovered quite recently that Japanese snow monkeys regularly bask in hot springs to gain extra warmth in their freezing habitat.

Two-year-old Squirrel Monkey about to embark on a flight.

Guinea-pig monkeys

ANCIENT philosophers were interested in the primates because of their obvious close relationship to human beings, but not until towards the end of the last century did scientists begin to make a really close study of monkeys. Then one of their main aims was to get more idea of the functioning of the human brain. Later, monkeys were used more and more in experimental work to find out about certain diseases that affect humans, and how they are spread. Domestic animals, particularly laboratory rats and mice, are used for some research work, but for other experiments it is necessary to use animals that are more closely related to man. The primates have therefore been the most suitable "guineapigs", and in recent years they have proved invaluable for testing drugs before these are used on human beings. It is appropriate to mention this here, because the majority of monkeys used in research have been Macaques and Baboons.

The late nineteen fifties and early sixties saw the largest trade in monkeys for research, as this was when vaccines for the prevention of poliomyelitis were being tested. In a three-year period during that time two hundred thousand monkeys were imported every year into the United States. More recently the number has dropped to fifty thousand per year. The most distressing aspects of this trade in its early years were the poor conditions and treatment to which many of the monkeys were subjected between being caught and arriving at their final destination. Many died through being overcrowded in their shipping boxes, particularly those that were in poor health to start with.

Most of these research monkeys were exported from India, and they were mainly Rhesus Macaques. Young, half-grown monkeys were most suitable for export as they travelled better and cost less in air freight charges, and these were extensively trapped in some parts of India. Because of this the balance of nature in their habitat was upset, as there were too few young Rhesus left to mature (and eventually breed) to keep the monkey populations at their normal level. Inevitably, there came a time when the remaining monkeys were too old to breed and there were few young ones to replace them. This created what is termed an "imbalance of populations".

Other primates have been used for research work too – the Pig-tailed Macaque, for instance, has been sent into space in rockets. After the Rhesus, however, the Crab-eating Macaque is probably the most popular. Baboons have played an increasingly important part in laboratory research recently, mainly because their blood circulatory systems are similar to those of humans. They are also useful for studying how diet affects the workings of the heart. Baboons have been used in kidney transplant work too, as their kidneys have been found to be more suitable for this than those of any other primates.

As most of the countries that supply laboratory monkeys have introduced export quotas, scientists have been forced to find alternative sources. Squirrel monkeys are now in great demand from South America, particularly by laboratories in the United States, as it is much cheaper for them to acquire monkeys from a country so near at hand.

Rhesus Monkey having its brain activity measured.

The leaf monkeys

Monkeys of the rain forests

THE LEAF-EATING monkeys are the most specialized feeders of all the primates, and have large, complex stomachs capable of holding food weighing one third of the monkeys' whole weight. These stomachs are not like ours, with a single compartment, but are divided into several smaller ones rather like the stomachs of the ruminants (cud-chewing animals). Whereas other monkeys have to search through the trees for one that is fruiting, leaf-eaters always have a plentiful supply of food to hand, and their modified digestive system enables them to get all the nourishment they need from foliage alone. Most leaf-eaters live in the tropical rain forests, which are evergreen – although their foliage is not like that of evergreen trees in northern regions. The trees in the rain forests are always in various stages of shedding their leaves, growing new ones, flowering and fruiting. Seen from the air, these forests look like a dense green carpet whatever the time of year.

With the exception of the three African species of leaf-eaters – the Black and White, the Green and the Red Colobus – all these specialized monkeys live in the forests of southern Asia and Indonesia. Black and White Colobus Monkeys have suffered more than any other species from a world-wide demand for their skins. These are still used in the fur trade, although on a very small scale now compared with the end of the last century, when several hundred thousand skins were exported from Africa. Fortunately the fashion changed before these handsome monkeys were exterminated. There are many races of this species, but they all have long silky black fur, pure white bushy tails and capes of white fur that reach the ground. Unlike most of the Asiatic leaf-eaters, which are plentiful and unafraid of humans, Colobus Monkeys are very secretive and are seldom

PETER JACKSON

seen in the tree tops. This may seem peculiar in view of the strong tonal contrasts of their fur, but in fact their coats blend with the hanging mosses, lichens and areas of shadow to form an effective camouflage in the gloom of the thick forests. Only when they move do they give away their position, either to hunters who would shoot them for their pelts or to the large eagles that scan the tree tops for prey.

In Asia, Langurs are the typical leaf-eating monkeys, but although they are abundant in their natural habitat they are seldom seen in zoos because of their specialized food requirements. In India there are enormous numbers of Langurs, of which the

Presbytis Entellus, which often inhabits towns and villages in India and Pakistan, where it is held sacred and is not molested. This Langur may spend as much as 80% of its time on the ground, though it never goes too far away from trees.

most plentiful are the Entellus Langurs – a sacred species in the eyes of some castes. There is also another group of slightly smaller monkeys known as Purple-faced Langurs, which actually do have bright purple skin on their faces. These too are apparently sacred to the Hindus, but there are people of other religions who regularly hunt them.

The feeling towards monkeys generally are frequently contradictory in southern Asia. Many are killed for their flesh or fur, and in some regions for the bezoar stones they produce in their stomachs. The formation of these stones occurs in areas where there are heavy mineral deposits in the soil; the monkeys eat the soil to provide their mineral salt requirements, just as domestic cattle are given salt licks to complete their diet. Bezoars are small, hard stones, green in colour and shaped rather like almonds, which form in the monkeys' stomachs as a result of the accumulation of mineral residues. Some years ago there was a thriving trade in these stones, which were thought by the Chinese to have medicinal qualities. One species of Leaf Monkey from the Sunda Islands was practically exterminated to meet the demand for bezoar stones.

Dusky Leaf Monkeys have distinct white circles around their eyes, which give them a most unusual appearance. They also have white chins and upper lips and are otherwise grey – although their babies are a glorious golden colour for a few weeks after birth. These monkeys are one of the many species of Lutongs, which are all fairly large monkeys with a crest of hair on top of their heads, usually growing from a central whorl. Several species of Lutongs produce bezoars. A Lutong from North Vietnam has a golden head, white cheeks and a yellow throat, but is otherwise greenish-brown, while on the Mentawi Islands off the coast of Sumatra lives the Red-bellied Lutong, a very colourful animal with an orange stomach, white throat and cheeks and a black body. The young of this monkey are golden at birth, like the Dusky Leaf Monkey babies.

The Doucs or Painted Langurs also live in the

Douc Langur, found in Indo-China. Mottled grey in colouring, this monkey has a yellow face, hands and feet and other parts in black, white and chestnut.

forests of Vietnam, and in their bright colouring rival the Golden Lion Marmoset, the Red Uakari and the Mandrill. One race has bright yellow facial skin, brown crown, reddish cheek tufts and a black and yellow collar; the basic body colour is grey, with black hands and feet and white wrists and arms. Another race has a black face.

The classification of these monkeys, and of many of the other primates too, changes periodically as zoologists study each group in more detail. Only a few years ago the Leaf Monkeys, the Banded Leaf Monkeys and the Indian Langurs were separated into different *genera* (the plural of *genus,* which means a group of similar species that do not inter-breed). Now they are all included in the same genus. There will no doubt be another alteration to this arrangement as more zoologists are able to spend more time studying each group and gain new information, particularly about their anatomy. While the leaf-eaters are obviously all closely related, the classification of other monkeys is often more puzzling – all the Old World monkeys, for instance (the Macaques, the Langurs and the Baboons) are included in the same family.

Spectacled Langur and young. These animals are not often seen in captivity because of their specialized diet.

Proboscis Monkey climbing a tree. This monkey with the strange-shaped nose is found only on the Island of Borneo.

Strange-shaped noses

One Group of leaf-eating monkeys have the most unusual noses in the whole of the monkey kingdom. Of the four species the most familiar is the Proboscis Monkey, which has a three-inch-long, flat-topped nose that reaches its widest point in the middle and hangs below its owner's chin. The other species have snub noses in which the nostrils point forwards.

Proboscis Monkeys live only on the island of Borneo. They are quite large, the males having been known to weigh fifty pounds – twice as much as the females. The males have the longest noses, too, but the newly-born babies have upturned noses that show no indication that they will eventually grow so long and bulbous. Mature animals have pink faces that change to deep red when they are very hot or annoyed.

Zoologists have never been able to say with certainty why any monkey should have such an unusual nose, although it is generally believed to be connected with natural selection. Loosely, this means that female Proboscis Monkeys favour the males with the largest noses and select these as their mates, shunning small-nosed individuals. It is rather like our present-day deliberate selection of (and breeding from) the hens that lay most eggs, which eventually produces a breed of frequent layers. This, of course, takes far less time than evolution through natural selection. The Malay people, who have short noses and brown skins, apparently call the Proboscis Monkey the *Orang Blanda* (meaning White Man) because of its long nose and pink complexion.

Like Rhesus Macaques, Proboscis Monkeys are expert swimmers and are seldom found far from water. They have been seen enjoying long swimming sessions in the rivers of Borneo, followed by equally long periods of sunbathing, as though resting after their earlier exertions. When moving through the forest gathering the leaves that form their basic diet they often find it necessary to cross rivers, and have no hesitation in leaping straight from the trees into the water. The Chinese are said to eat these monkeys, but they are still quite plentiful and are protected in Sarawak and North Borneo.

One Species of Snub-nosed Monkey lives on the islands off the southern coast of Sumatra. Unlike the other leaf-eaters this monkey has a short, hairless tail about six inches long, so it has appropriately been called the Pig-tailed Langur. It has short hands and feet, but its fingers and toes are very long. Another species, the Tonkin Snub-nosed Langur, lives in the forests of North Vietnam and resembles the Pig-tailed Langur except that it has a more upturned nose and a long, furred tail.

The last species is known simply as the Snub-nosed Monkey, and lives in the evergreen temperate forests of Burma and China. There are several races of this species, of which the Golden Monkey is the most colourful. Basically golden orange, it has a blue face and years ago its long, silky fur was used to weave robes for the Chinese Mandarins. Another race, called Brelich's Monkey, is deep brown and has a cape of white fur hanging from its shoulders. It lives only in the mountains of central China.

Head of a Proboscis Monkey, showing the strange nose formation. In old males this is especially enormous, and is also inflatable.

Head of a young Hanuman Langur, the sacred monkey of India and Ceylon.

Map showing location of Hanuman Langurs.

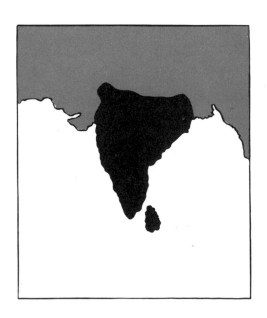

Sacred monkeys

India is the land of the monkey gods, and of these the most sacred is the leaf-eating Entellus, or Hanuman Langur. Recently it has been estimated that there are almost a hundred and fifty million Hanuman Langurs in India, all enjoying the freedom of that drought-stricken sub-continent. Certain towns – Benares, for example – are plagued by large numbers of these long-legged, grey-furred animals. The Hindus believe that Hanuman was the monkey ally of the great god Rama, so all Hanumans enjoy complete protection from human interference. To kill one is a sin of the worst kind, and at one time would have been avenged by devout Hindus. Thousands of years ago, even before this legend began, Hanumans were the guardian gods of Indian villages; when a new village was founded, the first essential was to make offerings to these gods.

Hanuman Langurs now wander the country as they wish, plundering the crops and stealing from villages and even from towns. Recently, however, there have been increasing demands – particularly from irate farmers – for a reduction in their numbers. Shooting has been suggested, but this is strongly opposed by the religiously-minded. Other plans have been put forward, based on the idea of driving the monkeys away from heavily-populated areas. One such plan was designed to affect the behaviour of the troops, which apparently disband if their leader is no longer acceptable to them. Troop leaders were caught and shaved all over, then allowed to rejoin their groups. In that condition they did prove unacceptable as leaders, and the troops disbanded; however, they simply dispersed to cause trouble elsewhere. Official monkey catchers were also employed, their task being to catch as many Hanumans as they could and transfer them to an area some distance away. This, of course, did not solve the problem either!

Other Leaf Monkeys are also sacred in the eyes of certain peoples; the Golden Monkey, for instance, is regarded with awe by many Chinese villagers. In West Africa Colobus Monkeys are thought to be the messengers of gods, and are protected by some tribes. These monkeys have the same habit of sunning themselves in the tree tops that has led to several species of Lemurs being regarded as sacred. Some of the Macaques, too, are thought to be sacred. The Rhesus Macaque has already been mentioned, and the original three wise monkeys were also Macaques – the Japanese species. These three wise monkeys, which feature in Buddhist teachings about the three main temptations of man, were originally carved above the door of the royal stables in some temples at Nikko in Japan. Their names are *Mizaru,* who sees no evil, *Kikazaru,* who hears no evil and *Iwazaru,* who speaks no evil. They were carved by the great Japanese woodcarver Jingoro, who died in 1652.

On the island of Celebes the Black Ape is revered by the coastal tribes in the north; They put food on rafts and float it downstream as an offering to this god, which they worship.

Hanuman Langurs with young. These monkeys are white or pale greyish in colour, and have black feet, hands and face. They also have large overhanging eyebrows of stiff hair.

Chimpanzee. These animals take about nine to twelve years to mature, and live in family groups consisting of an adult male, one or several females, infants and partly-grown young.

The apes

Our closest animal relatives

THE HIGHLY-DEVELOPED brains of apes give them an intelligence that surpasses that of all the other members of the animal kingdom, except man. They also differ from the other primates in having exceptionally long arms and no tails, and in being able to walk upright for varying distances, according to species. The Great Apes – Chimpanzees, Orang-Utans and Gorillas – are the most intelligent, followed by the Gibbons or Lesser Apes.

Just how intelligent are the apes? To begin with, it is difficult to define intelligence even in man, for it is a complex combination of many different things – the ability to learn, to acquire skills, to communicate and to solve problems, among others. It can explain why, for example, some people are better than others at doing certain jobs, or why some children are able to learn faster than others. In trying to assess the intelligence of apes we cannot even consider the most important aspect of human intelligence – the ability to learn a vocabulary. Literally thousands of tests have been devised to measure the mental capacity of apes; and although these have had to be carried out in rather artificial conditions, this is not necessarily a disadvantage.

Apes have scored highly in those simple tests and tasks which have stimulated their natural curiosity and made use of their great manual dexterity. They have even been able to solve problems by themselves, without training or assistance, especially when rewards have been offered. An example of this is provided by the Chimpanzees whose owner gave them some food inside a metal pipe. They managed to push out the food with splinters of wood that they had broken off a plank just for this purpose. In the San Diego Zoo, all the apes have been given simple tests. One of these involved dipping a thick rope through a small opening into a container of fruit juice, which they then sucked off; others involved drawing food into their cages with "tools". The Chimpanzees were quick to learn, but the Bonobos or Pygmy Chimpanzees were even quicker.

The Great Apes have a strong natural desire to explore and to try out all kinds of new things, but in the wild this is thwarted by the need to stay within the confines of the colony, or the family group. As baby apes grow and try to satisfy their inquisitive natures, they are restricted and disciplined by the laws of their society. In captivity, however, young apes have been able to concentrate fully on the intelligence tests, without fear of being punished by their elders and with an ease of mind no ape could achieve in the wild. Chimps and Gorillas have been given painting tests that proved that they have a basic sense of composition and are able to control their "painting". The zoologist Desmond Morris found that the urge to paint was so strong in young Chimpanzees that they did it willingly, without being trained or rewarded; Congo, the famous Chimpanzee at London Zoo, produced many paintings. Apes, particularly Chimpanzees, have also been trained to perform elaborate acts in the circus ring, and those used in American space research learned to use very elaborate instruments during space flights.

Chimpanzee showing intelligence in design. This ape also has a great sense of rhythm, shown by a kind of dance it performs and by its drumming on trees or on the ground.

RUSS KINNE

Acrobats of the jungle

Gibbons or Lesser Apes are confined to the Oriental region, from the eastern edge of the Himalayas to Sumatra, Java and Borneo, and their hooting calls are the most characteristic sounds of the monsoon forests. In many areas they are still hunted – sometimes for their fat, as this is thought to be a cure for rheumatism when rubbed into stiff joints. Also, just as some tribes eat tiger meat to make them as strong and wily as tigers, so Gibbons are eaten in the hope that their agility will be passed on to their hunters. The Malays in particular are very superstitious about these apes, and believe they have the power of both good and evil.

A monkey (above) usually has a tail. N

Gibbons are more specialized for life in the trees than the other apes, and they move by means of a long-armed, swinging movement known as brachiation. They swing by alternate arms with their legs dangling loosely below them, and with a flying leap they can clear gaps of twenty feet between the trees. On the ground they run with their arms held above their heads, but if they need to go very fast they usually drop on to all fours. Unlike the Great Apes, they do not make nests to sleep in. They have the reputation of being very charming animals and highly suitable for keeping as house pets, yet they are very excitable and unreliable and there have been many instances of their attacking their owners for no apparent reason. In the wild state they hoot continuously to keep neighbouring troops out of their territory, just as the Howler Monkeys do in South America. They also fight ferociously on occasions. In zoos they are just as territorially minded, and strange Gibbons introduced into a cage that the original occupants regard as their territory are immediately attacked. Gibbons' agility makes them fearsome adversaries, for they can make rapid attacks during which they give slashing bites with their sharp, recurved teeth.

Gibbons' coats are thick and woolly, rather like the fleece of sheep, and they are impervious to the

NEAVE PARKER

, such as a gibbon (below), has a tail.

heavy rainfalls of the monsoon regions. After a downpour they lick the water off their fur, although their normal way of drinking is to dip their hands into water that has collected in tree cavities, or on large leaves, and then lick the excess from their fur. Like the other apes they cannot swim, and if they are completely immersed they soon become waterlogged. Green nuts (rather like green almonds) are said to form a large part of their diet, and they also eat fruits, berries, leaves, shoots and flowers. The meat part of their diet consists of insects, tree-living frogs, snails and small lizards, and nestling birds and eggs. With their great ability and speed, Gibbons are sometimes even able to catch birds in flight.

Many contradictory names have been given to the different species of Gibbons since they were first discovered. To confuse matters even more, the species often occur in several colour phases in the same area, and sometimes males and females of the same species have different body colouring. Some even change colour when they mature. In fact, however, the seven species of Gibbons are quite easily identified by means other than colour, as each has a characteristic feature. In the case of the largest species, the Siamang – which is almost three feet tall and has an extra-long arm span – the identifying feature is its long and rather shaggy black coat. Siamangs are also unusual for two other reasons, the first being that both sexes have a large vocal sac, reddish-brown in colour, which can be inflated to increase the volume of sound when they whoop. When not in use, these sacs lie deflated and hidden in the thick fur of the neck. The second reason is that, while Siamangs are similar in shape to the other Gibbons, they differ from them in having webbing between the second and third toes.

In the Concolor Gibbons only the males have a throat sac, but the main identification feature of this species is their crests. The hair on top of the males' heads grows straight upwards to form one central spiky crest, where as the females have two distinct crests. One race of this species, found in Thailand, also has pure white whiskers. Like many of the Gibbons, Concolors have a wide range of colour phases, from black to golden, so the name Black Gibbon which they have recently been given is not altogether appropriate. If an alternative name to Concolor is needed, Crested Gibbon would be the most suitable. There is in any case another species of black gibbon, the Hoolock Gibbon, which can be recognized by the thick white band across its forehead, rather like heavy eyebrows. In old age Hoolocks often turn grey and sometimes buff, and their young are grey at birth.

Lar Gibbons have a wide distribution from Burma to the tip of the Malay peninsula, and are the species of Gibbon most frequently seen in zoos. They vary in colour from black to buff, their faces are encircled by a white ring and they have white hands and feet. Agile Gibbons have several colour phases too, but their feet are always the same colour as their bodies. They have a white facial ring, although in the pale-coloured forms this is barely lighter than the body. Moloch Gibbons are also confusingly called Grey, Silver and Wau-Wau Gibbons, yet neither of the names referring to their colour is acceptable as this species also has several other colour phases. Curiously enough, these Gibbons can most easily be identified by their lack of distinguishing features. They do not have light facial rings, brow bands, crests or white hands. The seventh species is known as the Dwarf Gibbon or Dwarf Siamang. As far as we know, it lives only on islands in the Mentawi Archipelago off the southern coast of Sumatra. It resembles a miniature Siamang, but has less webbing between its toes.

There is a legend amongst the Dyaks of Borneo that tells how Gibbons are supposedly descended from a man who always cooked over a very smoky fire. He eventually became ashamed because his face was encrusted with soot, and ran away and clung to the branches for so long that his arms stretched. Since that day, the legend says, all Gibbons have had black faces and long arms.

Gibbon. The remarkable vocal powers of this ape enable it to make itself heard over a distance of several miles. Gibbons sit upright, and when on the ground run in an erect position.

Young Orang Utan, which lives in the swampy coastal forests of Borneo and Sumatra.

RUSS KINNE

The old man of the woods

Orang Utans are the only Great Apes to survive outside Africa, and they are now found only in the lowland swampy forests of Borneo and Sumatra. The name Orang Utan is derived from Malayan words meaning "wild man", and the animal is often known in western countries as the wild man or the old man of the woods. In most areas where Orangs live they are known by local names, of which one of the most widely used is Mias.

Orangs are now uncommon everywhere and there are probably less than five thousand alive in the wild state. One of the major threats to their survival has been the increasing demand by zoos for baby Orangs, because the only way to obtain these is to shoot the mothers and then "rescue" the young ones and bottle-rear them. It would be difficult to catch the adults, and they probably would not take kindly to captivity. Unfortunately, the poor treatment received by baby Orangs between being captured and arriving at their final destination has accounted for many lives; it has been estimated that only one in every twenty babies survives the ordeal. At this rate of extermination it is not surprising that Orang Utan populations have dwindled during this century – their breeding rate could not possibly keep pace with the annual loss of youngsters and adult females. Fortunately, Orangs are now protected. To stop their being smuggled out of Borneo and Sumatra, responsible zoos all over the world have agreed not to buy the babies unless they have been legally exported, so trade in these apes has virtually ceased. Tom and Barbara Harrison of the Sarawak Museum have long been concerned about the traffic in Orangs and, largely due to their efforts, an Orang Utan rehabilitation centre has been established in the Bornean jungle. Here young Orangs that have been confiscated after illegal capture are released and carefully guarded while they learn how to survive in the jungle, which normally their parents would have taught them. To aid the conservation programme, Orangs are now being encouraged to breed in zoos throughout the world.

Orang Utans are second only to Gorillas in size and, as both Chimpanzees and Gorillas seek much of their food on the forest floor, Orangs are the largest animals to spend all their time in the trees. Males can weigh as much as two hundred pounds, but despite this they are remarkably agile; swinging under the branches in the same way as Gibbons, they can move very fast when the occasion demands. Normally, however, they are ponderous climbers and very deliberate in their movements. When they venture to the ground, which they rarely do in the wild, they are awkward and can only walk upright for short distances. Like Chimpanzees, their usual way of walking is on all fours, but when they need to move quickly along the ground they use their arms almost like crutches, swinging their legs between them.

Orangs have the most unusual appearance of all the apes, as everything about them seems to be out of proportion – their legs are short and weak, their heads are very large and they have extra wide shoulders which gives them a barrel-chested appearance. Their long, powerful forearms are capable of supporting their bulk for considerable periods, but their hands, with their long fingers and small thumbs, look quite human. In contrast, their big toes are shorter than the rest of their toes. As they age, Orangs become inactive and often develop pot-bellies. Adult males have large cheek pads, concave faces, piggy eyes, pimply skin and bridgeless noses that seem to sink back into their circular faces. They are clad in handsome reddish hair that may grow to almost a foot long, and they have long, drooping moustaches. Often in zoos there are individuals that are almost bald; this condition may be caused by a deficiency in their diet or possibly by boredom – for want of anything else to do they sometimes start plucking their hair out. Also, when they are kept in very artificial conditions, with rough concrete everywhere, their hard, abrasive sur-

Orang Utan and baby. These are large apes and this baby could eventually grow to over four feet in height.

roundings are likely to rub off their coats. Compared with the boisterous Chimpanzees, Orangs look relaxed at all times, and seem to live a calm, orderly life free from tension and worry.

Orang Utans have enormous jaws that are wider in front than at the back. These are very similar to Gorillas' jaws, and are immensely powerful for biting and crunching. This may seem an unusual adaptation for animals with a purely vegetable diet, but Orangs are in fact rather specialized feeders. For instance, they have been seen stripping the bark from trees with their teeth, and one of their main food items for part of the year is said to be the fruit of the Durian tree. These large fruits are filled with stringy pulp and many stones, and are very hard on the outside – so much so that the Malays have to strike them several blows with a sharp machete to expose their contents. It is hardly surprising that Orang Utans need powerful jaws to break them open.

One of the most peculiar features of this ape is the large throat pouch which extends over its shoulders and around its neck, and which can be inflated. The purpose of this pouch is not clear, and many suggestions have been made to account for its presence. One theory is that it may help to cushion the weight of the Orang's head while it is biting into thick-skinned fruit.

Although they are apparently no longer hunted for food, there was a time when Orang Utans played an important part in the diet of the Dyaks of Borneo, who killed them with poisoned darts fired from blow pipes. The hunters then had to cut the flesh away from the wound before eating the meat to avoid poisoning themselves. Once the Dyaks had located the Orangs in the forest they were assured of several targets, as Orangs live in family parties. These are strictly territorial and may roam the same area for many years. Occasionally, however, old males have been seen on their own, and sometimes several females and their babies have been seen together. Really, very little is known about the behaviour of

Orangs in the wild as they are so arboreal, but it is known that they make beds every evening to sleep in. They bend branches over to make the base of the nest, and then pile small broken branches and leaves on top of this to form a "mattress". It is also said that they make a cover for themselves with additional foliage, or snuggle down into the mattress if this is deep enough. The reason they make fresh beds every evening is that their rovings during the daytime normally take them some distance from the previous night's resting place. In zoos they are usually given a pile of straw or wood wool every evening to make their nests, and no matter how warm and draught-free their quarters are they always cover themselves completely with this bedding.

Male Orang Utan, with cheek-flanges. Only the male develops these flanges, the function of which is unknown. There is a great deal of facial variation amongst Orangs; they are as individual and instantly recognizable as human beings.

RUSS KINNE

Tea-party favourites

Unarmed, a young English zoologist named Jane Goodall recently lived for three and a half years amongst wild Chimpanzees in order to study their movements and habits. At first the Chimpanzees were wary of her presence and kept at a safe distance, but after several months they allowed her to get within a hundred yards of the colony. She even began to sleep close by when the Chimps settled down for the night, and was eventually accepted by them almost as a member of the troop. One animal became so friendly that he visited her camp and allowed himself to be groomed, this being the first recorded friendly contact between a wild ape and a human being. Jane Goodall studied these Chimpanzees for over three thousand hours, and not only brought back a wealth of new information on the life of wild Chimpanzees, but also proved that the old way of approaching them (armed to the teeth, and even caged for protection from "vicious attacks") was worse than useless.

In their natural habitat Chimpanzees have been seen to eat small animals, although those Chimps that live in the dense forests are thought to eat mainly large insects to provide the meat part of their diet. In the more open forests, Chimps have been seen to eat young antelope, bush pig and, on one occasion, a Colobus Monkey, which they shared without squabbling amongst themselves. Despite this, however, they are basically vegetarians, eating a wide variety of nuts, fruit, leaves, shoots, flowers, juicy plant stems and bark.

Chimpanzees live in family parties and, apart from being terrorized by the occasional leopard, have little fear from wild animals. They are terrified of snakes, however small, but their worst enemy is man (although there is no record of Chimps ever having been hunted for their flesh). Still the most plentiful of the Great Apes, Chimpanzees' numbers have been seriously reduced in recent years by the advance of settlements and cultivation into their territories, and by the shooting of females to obtain babies. Although they build nests at night, they do not seem to make roofs to provide shelter from the rain, and they frequently have to sit through torrential downpours. Another interesting feature of their sleeping habits is that adults never share their beds, and only small babies are allowed to share their mothers' nests. These nests are built like those of the Orangs with branches pulled in, and broken if necessary, to form a platform, after which others are pulled around to form a rim. Sometimes Chimpanzees build their nests on the ground, in which case safety rims are unnecessary.

Chimpanzees spend most of their time on the ground, searching for food, and climb trees only to collect specific fruit, to escape danger and, generally, to sleep. In shape and behaviour they are a complete contrast to the Orangs. They are smaller – adult males weighing about a hundred pounds and females slightly less – but they are immensely strong and are more than a match for the average man. They do not have the barrel chests of the Orangs, and their arms are shorter, but their legs are longer and their black hair is far less luxuriant. Their faces vary considerably in conformation; they are, in fact, as varied as those of humans. On the ground Chimpanzees walk on all fours with their hands

Opposite: baby Chimpanzee, showing off its hanging skill. Below: Chimpanzee drinking. Almost human in many ways, the Chimpanzee can become very friendly indeed.

almost closed, so that the weight of the shoulders is carried on the knuckles, and their feet are placed flat. In this position they can move very fast. They can also stand upright on their hind limbs, but they seldom do so, and although they are expert climbers and can brachiate like the Gibbons they prefer to travel on the forest floor. Chimpanzees cross rivers or chasms by hurling themselves from overhanging trees into the foliage of trees on the other side, where they land with a great crash.

Chimpanzees are the most expressive apes, and "talk" among themselves with a variety of facial expressions and loud cries. They are probably the rowdiest of all animals, and as well as their wide vocabulary and their lip-smacking and pouting they have developed many means of making noises. Chest beating, tree drumming and foot stamping are all employed by them and may last for several hours, interspersed by bouts of whooping and yelling. It is not clear why they should act in this way, but it may be connected with defence of their territory. They also tear up clumps of earth and vegetation and hurl these at intruders, often with very good aim. Several investigators of Chimpanzees in the Congo forests have said that this sort of display also occurs when wandering bands of Chimps meet, and is no doubt a form of threat and counter-threat.

In captivity Chimpanzees have lived for over thirty years, and it is thought that their full life-span may be in the region of fifty years. When young they are often used to take part in tea parties, but they usually get out of hand as they mature. They have been bred more frequently in zoos than any other ape, and it has sometimes been necessary to hand rear them when their mothers were unable or unwilling to care for them. They have even been raised along with human babies, but though the Chimpanzee babies developed faster for the first few years, they then fell behind their more advanced relatives.

A Chimpanzee was the first anthropoid ape to be brought to Europe, although at the time it was called an Orang Utan. The first anatomical comparison of a

Chimpanzee. This ape is not only human in expression and gesture, it also has twelve ribs just as human beings do. Chimpanzees are found in every zoo and the young are a particular delight to children.

Chimpanzee and a human being was made towards the end of the seventeenth century by a leading London physician, who reported that the Chimpanzee resembled man far more closely than any of the monkeys that he also studied.

South of the Congo river in central Africa there is another species or subspecies of Chimpanzee that is a rare animal in the natural state. Only discovered about forty years ago, it was thought to be just a small race of Chimpanzee. However, some zoologists now regard it as a separate species and call it the Bonobo or Pygmy Chimpanzee. Less than half the size of the "standard model" when adult, it has a slender build and narrow shoulders and its ears are smaller and its head more rounded. It is said to be much more sensitive and placid than its larger relative, rarely biting or flying into a rage. The Bonobo's calls are also different, and its second and third toes are partially joined. It is now thought that this ape bears the closest resemblance to man, both in structure and in behaviour.

Gorillas

Until quite recently, Gorillas were sadly misrepresented animals. The first descriptions brought back to civilization by the early explorers and hunters all emphasized their ferocity, and dramatic reports were written of huge male Gorillas savagely attacking the intrepid explorers, all the time beating their chests and roaring with rage. They were reputedly so powerful that, even after being struck by several bullets, they could still seize the nearest gunbearers and tear them limb from limb before succumbing to their wounds. It is hardly surprising that for many years the world thought of Gorillas as savage beasts of prey. Even in this century, an American film company entered the jungle equipped with huge cages to protect their camera crews from Gorilla attacks while they tried to film them.

Only recently have these false impressions been corrected by zoologists who have studied Gorillas in their forest homes. One of these, an American named George Schaller, found that the most successful way of observing Gorillas was to enter their territory alone and unarmed; and although wild Gorillas are far more nervous than Chimpanzees, they allowed him to approach within fifty yards of them. They were at ease when he was clearly in view and became very nervous and excited when they lost sight of him but, even though some individuals approached to within a few feet of him, he was never attacked.

Paul du Chaillu was the first European to kill a Gorilla – or, at least, the first to announce that he had done so. It happened about the middle of the last century, and there were hysterical scenes when he produced skins and skeletons of Gorillas to prove that these huge "wild men" really existed. Many did not believe his stories, and some even doubted that he had ever been to Africa. Towards the end of the century, when the presence of these Great Apes in the western forests had been proved beyond doubt, a German explorer in the forests high on Mount Sabino on the eastern edge of the Congo shot a Gorilla which proved to be different from the western specimens. It is now accepted that there are two races of Gorilla – one in the northern Congo, Cameroons, Gabon, Chad and the Central African Republic, and the other in an area of mountainous, heavily forested country bordering Uganda and Tanzania. These races have been named the Lowland Gorilla and the Mountain Gorilla respectively (though many groups of the Lowland race also live in mountain forests). Like Chimpanzees, Gorillas show a great deal of facial variation and no two look exactly alike. There is also a considerable resemblance to each other among the members of any Gorilla family.

The Gorilla is the largest and most impressive of all the primates. Adult males can weigh over six hundred pounds, and a specimen in the Natural History Museum in London measures nine feet from finger tips to finger tips across the front of its body. In life it would have stood six feet tall. Gorillas differ in many respects from the other apes, particularly in their rather pointed heads and small ears, their enormous neck and shoulder muscles and their large, flared nostrils which point upwards. When

Above: Bukhama, the 16-stone Gorilla at Dudley Zoo in Worcestershire. Opposite and below: Guy, at London Zoo.

mature they have a prominent crest at the base of the skull, rising high above the head. They can stand upright on their hind limbs but prefer to walk on all fours, using the knuckles to support the weight of the torso. They live in family parties, and some individuals bear the scars of injuries received in family arguments, when tusk-like canine teeth were used to good effect.

Some central African tribes regard Gorillas as their guardian spirits and treat them with great respect, but others look on them purely as food. The wildlife photographer Armand Denis found that a certain tribe relied on Gorillas not only for the bulk of their meat supplies, but also for their sport and excitement. They regarded Gorillas almost as rival tribesmen, and frequently went out to hunt them with large nets that they spread around the area of forest in which the animals were sleeping. When the Gorillas tried to break through at daybreak, they were faced by several hundred tribesmen armed with guns and spears. Unfortunately, the tribesmen often went on killing the Gorillas long after they had enough meat. After the Orang Utan, the Gorilla is the ape most seriously threatened with extinction in the wild state, for as well as being hunted regularly for food it has also suffered from the political strife in its region in recent times. There are thought to be less than fifteen thousand Mountain Gorillas left, and the Lowland race numbers no more than fifty thousand.

Gorillas usually make a fast escape when alarmed, but sometimes the dominant male may turn to deliver his threat display. This is similar to that of the Chimpanzee, with a lot of chest beating, roaring and vegetation throwing; it is meant to intimidate the prospective enemy, and make him think twice about attacking or following the Gorillas. Apart from occasional leopard attacks, however, Gorillas have no natural enemies other than man. Unlike Orang Utans, that are deliberately shot to obtain their babies, it seems that the sale of baby Gorillas for eventual zoo exhibition is largely a by-product of

Gorilla hunting for the pot; the babies are kept alive simply because they have little value as meat animals.

The largest land mammals are all vegetarians, so it is hardly surprising to find that the largest primate lives solely on vegetable matter (just like the hippopotamus, the rhinoceros, the giraffe and the elephant). Gorillas' food intake is, naturally, enormous; they eat large amounts of bark, berries, shoots, seedlings and fibrous plants daily. They are particularly fond of young banana plants, and often raid plantations for these.

Baby Gorillas have occasionally been kept as house pets, but as they have matured their owners have usually found accommodation for them in zoos. In America an adult Gorilla kept as a pet used to help his owner with the washing-up, but one day he retaliated when she accidentally knocked him with a broom. Fortunately, a friend was on hand to stun the Gorilla with a saucepan and save its owner from more serious injury.

The Gorilla is the largest of the man-like apes, reaching a height of about 5½ feet. It makes its bed in the branches of trees, constructing a fresh bed each night. Because of their great weight some adult males have to sleep on the ground.

JAMES SIMON

Above: upper part of an Australopithecine man.

Below: Australopithecine skull, found in South Africa.

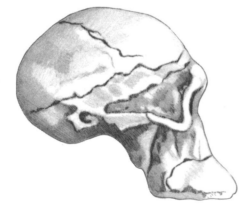

Almost human

WE SAW in the first pages of this book how the primitive insect-eating animals gave rise to the early primates, and then how, almost thirty million years ago, they evolved into the monkeys with long tails for balancing. These were followed by the long-armed, brachiating apes which had no use for tails when speeding through the branches. All these animals became specialized for existence in the great forests, but their increased size also made them less vulnerable on the ground and their visits to the forest floor became more frequent. However, they had no reason to abandon their aboreal way of life completely. On the ground there were already many highly-developed vegetarian animals with which they would have to compete for food. There were also innumerable carnivorous animals which would threaten their existence.

In the South American forests the primates developed no further than the specialized hand-tailed monkeys, but in the tropical forests of the Old World some evolved into apes. Even before they reached this point, however, their forests were being greatly reduced by changes in the world's climate. Some primates stayed on in the diminished forests and developed into the apes as we know them today.

Others left the jungles to colonize the grasslands and, despite competition from animals already adapted for that environment, they somehow managed to evolve into the most intelligent animals on earth – human beings.

While it is therefore correct to say that we evolved from the apes, it would be quite wrong to think that we are direct descendants of Gorillas and Chimpanzees. It is generally agreed that we had common ancestors in the very early apes, but the apes and man went their separate ways about fifteen million years ago.

Our ancestors were not adapted for grazing as the early herbivores were, nor were they killers like the early carnivores, so to begin life in the grasslands they had to grub about in the soil for roots and bulbs, and gather seeds and berries. To provide the meat part of their diet they no doubt ate grubs, the eggs and nestlings of ground dwelling birds and weak or injured animals that could be easily caught – much the same omnivorous diet, in fact, as during their life in the trees. This arrangement went on for several million years, but all the time a gradual improvement was taking place in their food gathering ability. As they were animals with well-developed brains, good eyesight and strong grasping hands, it was only natural that they should eventually develop a more upright stance to increase their speed for hunting. Once their hands were no longer needed to help them run they found they could throw stones and other objects at their prey, and from this developed the use of weapons and improved hunting techniques. Their need to survive was obviously urgent, and the continual desire to protect themselves and improve their means of obtaining food made the use of their brains more and more vital. Soon they began to think about making permanent homes instead of wandering over a large area like "wild animals", and once that had happened man was truly in the making.

Since Charles Darwin's time there has been a continual search for proof of this descent from the

Homo habilis eating grubs. Remains of this primitive man have been dated at over 2,000,000 years old.

apes in the form of skeletal remains. It is, after all, easy enough to show that the apes and man have certain similarities; you will remember that a London physician did this several centuries ago. But what has happened to all the animals that came between the apes and present day man – all the "missing links", as they have been called? Unfortunately, many are still missing. Several remains of early man have been discovered in parts of the Old World, but there are still many gaps in this evolutionary chain.

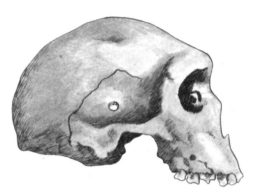

The most exciting finds in recent years, which have thrown considerable light on some of our nearest ancestors, have been unearthed by Dr. and Mrs. Louis Leakey in Tanzania. Until then the oldest human remains that had been located were those of *Australopithecus* in South Africa; these are thought to belong to a race that lived up to one million years ago. The Leakeys' discoveries in Olduvai Gorge in 1964, however, are thought to date from almost two million years ago. This race has been named *Homo habilis*. Other remains unearthed in the same region are similar to skulls and jaws discovered in Java and China, and belong to a more recent period of the earth's history. So from Tanzania we have a record of ancient man and how he lived from two million years ago until about five hundred thousand years ago. Along with remains unearthed elsewhere (in Italy and Israel, for example) which relate to more recent times, this provides a reasonably good record of our ancestors during the last two million years.

Above and below: Neanderthal man and his skull. Fossilized skulls of this kind of man have been discovered in many caves in Europe. They have been found to bear a marked resemblance to the skull of modern man, and especially to that of a 5-year-old child.

From then backwards to the time when we diverged from the apes there is only scanty evidence of the stages of our evolution, but probably before long fresh material for study will be unearthed by the palaeoanthropologists (who study the origin of man from fossil evidence). The remains of a creature called Proconsul, dating from the Miocene period about thirty million years ago, have been found. This creature is thought to provide evidence, even if it is rather vague, of a stage in the evolution of the long-

Above: Cro-magnon man, who appeared after Neanderthal man. Below: Cromagnon knife.

tailed monkeys into the tail-less apes, and is also thought to be very closely connected with the long-extinct primates that gave rise to man.

Dr Leakey's *Homo habilis* of two million years ago made crude tools for hunting and is thought, because of the shape of his jawbone, to have been able to speak. The size and shape of his teeth also indicate that he was a meat eater. Progressing to a mere thirty thousand years ago, there is ample evidence of the existence of a race of early man – Cromagnon Man – that evolved in Asia and moved westwards, killing off, it is believed, the less advanced Neanderthal Man. Cromagnon Man was a hunter of the giant mammoths; he wore animal skins, made tools and weapons from bones and placed his dead in shallow graves. He is considered to be the direct ancestor of the present day dolichocephalic (long-headed) peoples of western Europe. There is, for example, a resemblance between Cromagnon Man (as reconstructed from the remains found) and people at present living in Spain and the Canary Isles.

Acknowledgements

The sources of some of the photographs appearing in this volume are as follows: Bruce Coleman Limited, pages 31, 33, 45, 47, 50, 51, 52, 56, 57, 63, 70, 72 (*top*), 76, 80, 87. Popperfoto, pages 41, 49 (*top*), Zoological Society of London, page 64.

Index